ACTION PLANNER

ACTION PLANNER

Wield the Power of Your Will

This 26-week accountability tool uses a treatment plan approach for intentional wellness and goal achievement.

**By Nakeya T. Fields,
Licensed Clinical Social Worker**

Happy Woman | #1 Best-Selling Author | Creator | Speaker | Motivator | Consultant

Manifest it!

ACTION PLANNER

Wield the power of your will! This 26-week accountability tool uses a treatment plan approach for intentional wellness and goal achievement.

Names: Nakeya T. Fields, author.
Chell Le Carter, contributor. Amanda Gonzalez, contributor.
Title: Manifest it! Action Planner
Description: First edition|California: Atmosphere Publishing, 2024
ISBN 979-8-89132-220-2 (paperback)| ISBN 978-1-948568-03-6 (ebook)
Library of Congress Control Number: 2024914570
Subjects: Health, Mental Health, Self Help,
Personal Development

First Edition: May 2024

Limit of Liability/Disclaimer of Warranty

Table of Contents

CONNECT WITH THE
MANIFEST IT! COMMUNITY!

The Manifest it! Action Planner is intended to support the development and implementation of healthy wellness routines. Join our community of wellness aficionados and keep track of your wellness habits.

Enjoy the benefits of connecting to a community.

Leaders on the interactive board receive exclusive deals on the products, services, and experiences we need and love, as well as early access to exclusive content.

 Look for the medal throughout your planner as a reminder to accomplish and track your goals on the leaderboard.

manifestapothecary.com/connect

Week 1

BECOMING A CREATOR

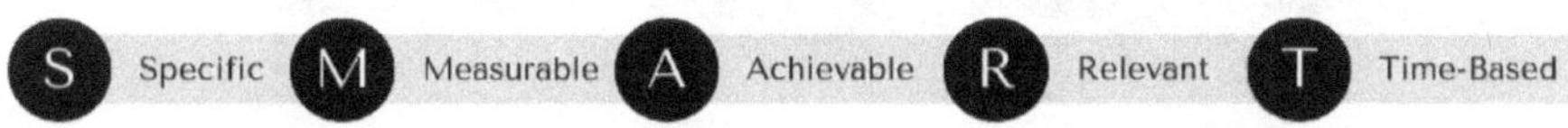

Use SMART Goals to create a self-care routine that is in alignment with the intended lifestyle change. Therapeutic, evidence-based practices have shown that setting SMART (specific, measurable, attainable, relevant, time-based) goals increases the likelihood of individuals meeting their goals and feeling accomplished.

We will practice identifying what is stopping us from accessing our personal power. We will manifest the life of our dreams with self-awareness, intention, action, and strength of will by speaking to self-esteem, building routine, and effecting positive self-talk.

GOAL OF THIS MOMENT

Identify 1-2 goals for this moment in time. Although the planner is a weekly accountability tool, time itself can keep us stuck in our worry about deadlines. It is encouraged that we choose a goal that we need completed each week that will make us feel the most productive and successful. Be specific and task oriented, as well as forgiving and loving of self.

Leonard, K. (2022, May 11). The Ultimate Guide to S.M.A.R.T. goals. Forbes. https://www.forbes.com/advisor/business/smart-goals/

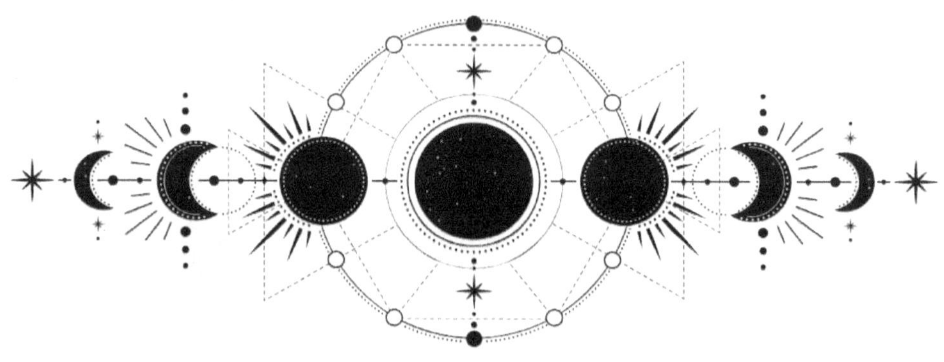

DATE:

SUNDAY
MONDAY
TUESDAY
WEDNESDAY
THURSDAY
FRIDAY
SATURDAY

THIS WEEK I AM MANIFESTING...

ACTION STEPS

What will be done by the end of the week?

TIMELINE   By when? (Day/Month)

RESPONSIBILITIES

Who will complete the prioritized tasks?

RESOURCES

(A) Resources Available (B) Resources Needed

COMMUNICATION PLAN

Who/What/When/Where/How
was it communicated?

POTENTIAL BARRIERS

What might cause resistance
to the ACTION STEPS? How?

GO GET IT MANTRA...

Choose a useful quote, image, or statement to serve as mental motivation. We must be loving of self when we choose this mantra.

GOAL OF THIS MOMENT

 TASK LIST

Write down 10 action items that will lead you to your goal.

ACCOMPLISHMENTS

Be loud, proud, and bold about the things we have been able to conquer this week. Cheer this moment, do a happy dance, and notice the tasks left behind, for they were always meant for next week's accomplishment section instead. Celebrate even the tiniest success and we will attract more.

HOW DOES YOUR BODY FEEL?

Take this moment to notice ourselves. Are we breathing? Notice if our bodies need to stretch, take a break, or get some fresh air. This accountability tool also serves to help us take care of ourselves. When needed, document exactly what you noticed from this moment and throughout this week. This will be useful to track stressors and triggers, which can be barriers to action steps.

⊛ SELF CARE CHECKLIST

- ☐ Take 10 Deep Breaths
- ☐ Move! (Walk, Yoga, Run, Strut)
- ☐ Listen to Your Favorite Music
- ☐ Aromatherapy Time-Out
- ☐ Indulge in a Favorite __________
- ☐ Scream Out Loud!
- ☐ __________________

- ☐ __________________
- ☐ __________________
- ☐ __________________
- ☐ __________________
- ☐ __________________
- ☐ __________________
- ☐ __________________

I AM...

FREE WRITE PAGE

Week 2

WHAT I WANT, WANTS ME

The Universe wants us to be happy and have what we want. Just like the moon, we are whole in all our phases. We are exactly where we are supposed to be in that cycle.

This reality is manifested by us alone. Only we have the ability to choose the thought that wins. Let's choose to know that we are in control of what we say, what we do, who we spend time with, and how we move. Boundaries with ourselves and others are necessary to stay in control of our internal and external domains.

Opening the throat chakra to speak our truth, at times, requires fortitude to stay sturdy in our lane. It's our lane to create and maintain. Staying on the path without distraction is the way of the powerful. We will not be moved.

HOMEWORK

Practice positive self talk daily. It is time to hold space to remind yourself of what you want to manifest. Think about how our environment and nature can impact our wellness routines. Here are some mantras/affirmations to consider.

SUGGESTED MANTRAS/AFFIRMATION STATEMENTS:

- I am safe, happy, and connected to others.
- I am a loving, beautiful, creative person and this is reflected in my relationships with others.
- I am confident in who I am. I love and accept myself every day.
- Wonderful new opportunities are opening up for me to use my unique creative skills and abilities.
- I attract only loving and uplifting people into my life.

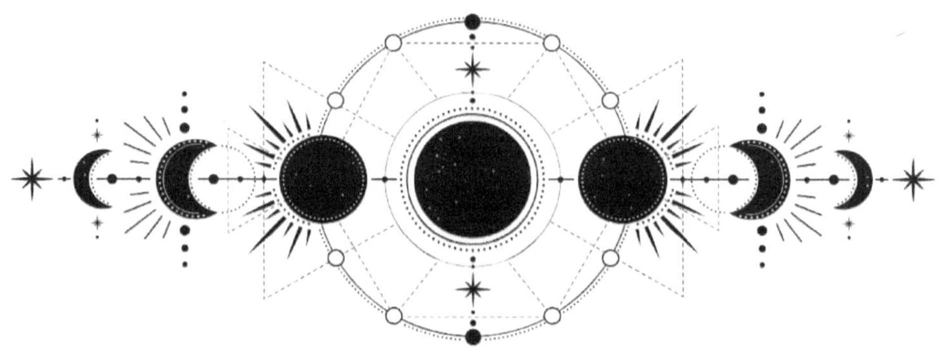

DATE:

SUNDAY
MONDAY
TUESDAY
WEDNESDAY
THURSDAY
FRIDAY
SATURDAY

THIS WEEK I AM MANIFESTING...

ACTION STEPS

What will be done by the end of the week?

TIMELINE   By when? (Day/Month)

RESPONSIBILITIES

Who will complete the prioritized tasks?

RESOURCES

(A) Resources Available (B) Resources Needed

COMMUNICATION PLAN

Who/What/When/Where/How was it communicated?

POTENTIAL BARRIERS

What might cause resistance to the ACTION STEPS? How?

GO GET IT MANTRA...

Choose a useful quote, image, or statement to serve as mental motivation. We must be loving of self when we choose this mantra.

GOAL OF THIS MOMENT

 TASK LIST

Write down 10 action items that will lead you to your goal.

ACCOMPLISHMENTS

Be loud, proud, and bold about the things we have been able to conquer this week. Cheer this moment, do a happy dance, and notice the tasks left behind, for they were always meant for next week's accomplishment section instead. Celebrate even the tiniest success and we will attract more.

HOW DOES YOUR BODY FEEL?

Take this moment to notice ourselves. Are we breathing? Notice if our bodies need to stretch, take a break, or get some fresh air. This accountability tool also serves to help us take care of ourselves. When needed, document exactly what you noticed from this moment and throughout this week. This will be useful to track stressors and triggers, which can be barriers to action steps.

⊛ SELF CARE CHECKLIST

- ☐ Take 10 Deep Breaths
- ☐ Move! (Walk, Yoga, Run, Strut)
- ☐ Listen to Your Favorite Music
- ☐ Aromatherapy Time-Out
- ☐ Indulge in a Favorite __________
- ☐ Scream Out Loud!
- ☐ __________________

- ☐ __________________
- ☐ __________________
- ☐ __________________
- ☐ __________________
- ☐ __________________
- ☐ __________________
- ☐ __________________

I AM...

FREE WRITE PAGE

Week 3

STAY READY, SO YOU DON'T HAVE TO GET READY

Are you a thinker too? Do you find that you sometimes cause your own suffering because of all the thoughts you believe and follow blindly?

If so, it's something of which to be aware. It takes discipline and self awareness to jump out of the patterns that don't serve us, and it starts with the way we think. Are we the master of our thoughts or are we the servants?

Let's claim the power position. We are the Masters. If we so choose to be.

What matters most is that we are trying for US. For our own hopes, dreams, aspirations, and comfort. We must be making effort always in favor of our "yes." Yes. We get to care about our own selves and make every effort to forgive and love ourselves for all parts of us: the god/goddess, the wild, the fragile, and the mess.

ACTIVITY

Create a list of activities or goals that you have always wanted to accomplish but never completed because of your own self-doubt. Write down the reasons you never completed those goals. Cross out the negative, self-deprecating reasons that no longer serve you. Take minor steps to complete the goals that have always been in the back of your mind.

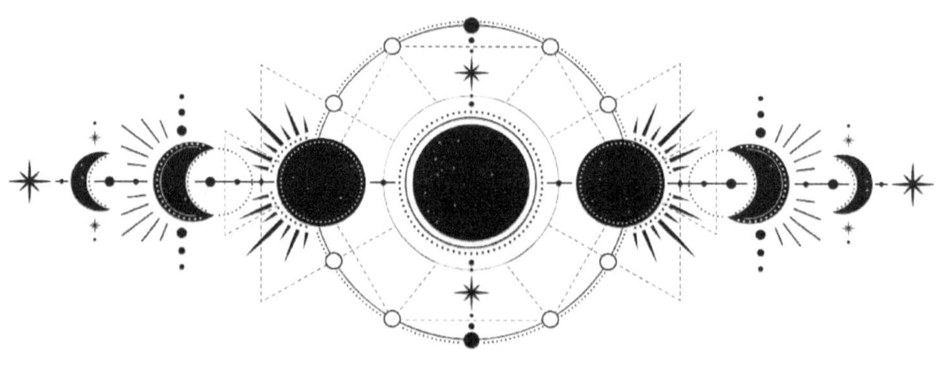

SUNDAY
MONDAY
TUESDAY
WEDNESDAY
THURSDAY
FRIDAY
SATURDAY

THIS WEEK I AM MANIFESTING...

ACTION STEPS

What will be done by the end of the week?

TIMELINE   By when? (Day/Month)

RESPONSIBILITIES

Who will complete the prioritized tasks?

RESOURCES

(A) Resources Available (B) Resources Needed

COMMUNICATION PLAN

Who/What/When/Where/How
was it communicated?

POTENTIAL BARRIERS

What might cause resistance
to the ACTION STEPS? How?

GO GET IT MANTRA...

Choose a useful quote, image, or statement to serve as mental motivation. We must be loving of self when we choose this mantra.

GOAL OF THIS MOMENT

 TASK LIST

Write down 10 action items that will lead you to your goal.

ACCOMPLISHMENTS

Be loud, proud, and bold about the things we have been able to conquer this week. Cheer this moment, do a happy dance, and notice the tasks left behind, for they were always meant for next week's accomplishment section instead. Celebrate even the tiniest success and we will attract more.

HOW DOES YOUR BODY FEEL?

Take this moment to notice ourselves. Are we breathing? Notice if our bodies need to stretch, take a break, or get some fresh air. This accountability tool also serves to help us take care of ourselves. When needed, document exactly what you noticed from this moment and throughout this week. This will be useful to track stressors and triggers, which can be barriers to action steps.

⊛ SELF CARE CHECKLIST

- ☐ Take 10 Deep Breaths
- ☐ Move! (Walk, Yoga, Run, Strut)
- ☐ Listen to Your Favorite Music
- ☐ Aromatherapy Time-Out
- ☐ Indulge in a Favorite __________
- ☐ Scream Out Loud!
- ☐ __________

- ☐ __________
- ☐ __________
- ☐ __________
- ☐ __________
- ☐ __________
- ☐ __________
- ☐ __________

I AM...

FREE WRITE PAGE

SAY 'YES' BUT KEEP 'NO' IN THE VOCABULARY GARDEN

Understanding how bravery to thrive through life transitions intersects with our ability to say no to that which does not serve our best interests is crucial to our growth.

We speak in power dynamics because we believe that we can call our power to us. We can call back our power from anyone we inadvertently gave it to when we thought they were someone we could trust and we can generate more of it when feeling energetically depleted. One way we can access the feeling of empowerment is through gratitude.

Did you know that when we practice gratitude, we experience significantly higher levels of happiness and psychological well-being? The data says so! Did you also know that when we focus on the good in life and acknowledge the moments of hope and joy, we are less depressed, less anxious, less stressed, and report having less symptoms of physical pain? Our ability to notice a positive moment or achievement also brings us more success at work and leads to higher self-esteem.

Gratitude is the answer. Today, I feel grateful for my experiences with water, my ability to make friends and be adventurous, and most of all...sunshine!

ACTIVITY

Create art! Create any form of art that moves you, inspires you, and reminds you of your greatness. Don't forget to display that work of art in a place where you will be able to see it and be proud.

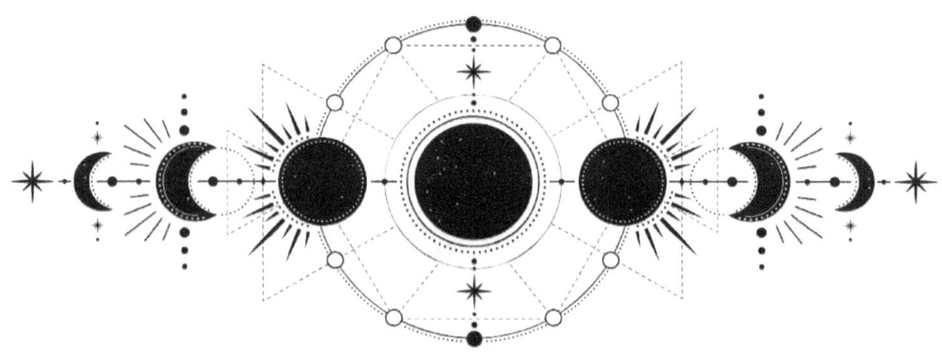

DATE:

SUNDAY
MONDAY
TUESDAY
WEDNESDAY
THURSDAY
FRIDAY
SATURDAY

THIS WEEK I AM MANIFESTING...

ACTION STEPS

What will be done by the end of the week?

TIMELINE   By when? (Day/Month)

RESPONSIBILITIES

Who will complete the prioritized tasks?

RESOURCES

(A) Resources Available (B) Resources Needed

COMMUNICATION PLAN

Who/What/When/Where/How was it communicated?

POTENTIAL BARRIERS

What might cause resistance to the ACTION STEPS? How?

GO GET IT MANTRA...

Choose a useful quote, image, or statement to serve as mental motivation. We must be loving of self when we choose this mantra.

GOAL OF THIS MOMENT

TASK LIST

Write down 10 action items that will lead you to your goal.

ACCOMPLISHMENTS

Be loud, proud, and bold about the things we have been able to conquer this week. Cheer this moment, do a happy dance, and notice the tasks left behind, for they were always meant for next week's accomplishment section instead. Celebrate even the tiniest success and we will attract more.

HOW DOES YOUR BODY FEEL?

Take this moment to notice ourselves. Are we breathing? Notice if our bodies need to stretch, take a break, or get some fresh air. This accountability tool also serves to help us take care of ourselves. When needed, document exactly what you noticed from this moment and throughout this week. This will be useful to track stressors and triggers, which can be barriers to action steps.

⊛ SELF CARE CHECKLIST

☐ Take 10 Deep Breaths	☐ _______________
☐ Move! (Walk, Yoga, Run, Strut)	☐ _______________
☐ Listen to Your Favorite Music	☐ _______________
☐ Aromatherapy Time-Out	☐ _______________
☐ Indulge in a Favorite _______	☐ _______________
☐ Scream Out Loud!	☐ _______________
☐ _______________	☐ _______________

I AM...

FREE WRITE PAGE

<h1 style="text-align:center">Week 5</h1>

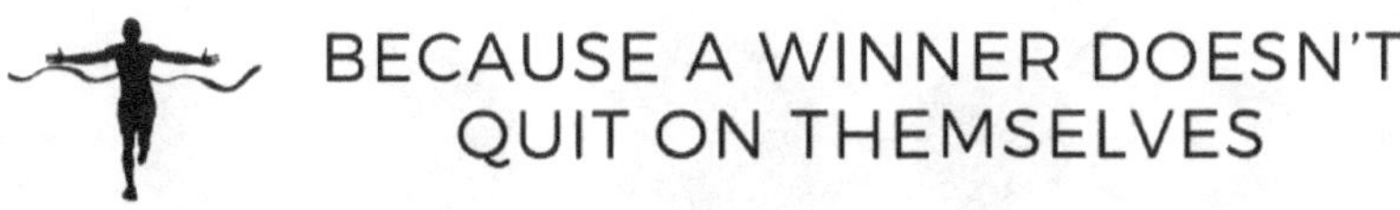

BECAUSE A WINNER DOESN'T QUIT ON THEMSELVES

Faith in self determines faith in the ability to take chances that feel uncomfortable. Explore some of the possible barriers to adding new practices to our daily routine.

In times of transition, we have a golden opportunity to create something new for ourselves and our routine: a whole shift of perspective with new things to notice and adjustments to get used to. We must change to evolve. The transition can be difficult, even painful. But in the end, we can fly. In the full moon we get the opportunity to let it go. Release it. Know first that you need to release "it", and then do so.

It all starts with awareness and ends with intention. Let us release that which does not serve us. Let us release the shadows that block our clarity and foresight. Let us release the trauma that keeps us in unhealthy patterns. Let us forgive the pain of past choices and release the guilt and worry; it does not reside here. We know the power of choice. We are powerful.

Journaling and affirmations help us to hone our intention. Practice. Practice. Practice. The moon cycle is enduring and a great way to help build a routine of awareness.

ACTIVITY

Create a nightly self-care routine. Anything that your heart desires: bubble baths, candles, facials, mantras, yoga, sound bath, etc.

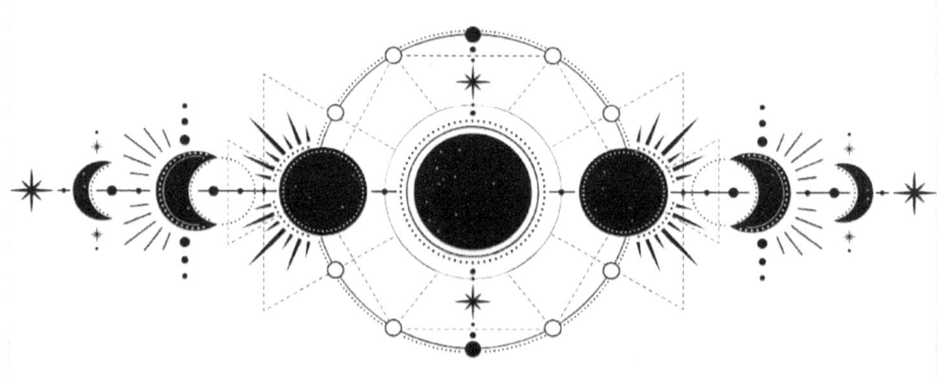

DATE:

SUNDAY
MONDAY
TUESDAY
WEDNESDAY
THURSDAY
FRIDAY
SATURDAY

THIS WEEK I AM MANIFESTING...

ACTION STEPS

What will be done by the end of the week?

TIMELINE   By when? (Day/Month)

RESPONSIBILITIES

Who will complete the prioritized tasks?

RESOURCES

(A) Resources Available (B) Resources Needed

COMMUNICATION PLAN

Who/What/When/Where/How was it communicated?

POTENTIAL BARRIERS

What might cause resistance to the ACTION STEPS? How?

Choose a useful quote, image, or statement to serve as mental motivation. We must be loving of self when we choose this mantra.

GOAL OF THIS MOMENT

TASK LIST

Write down 10 action items that will lead you to your goal.

ACCOMPLISHMENTS

Be loud, proud, and bold about the things we have been able to conquer this week. Cheer this moment, do a happy dance, and notice the tasks left behind, for they were always meant for next week's accomplishment section instead. Celebrate even the tiniest success and we will attract more.

HOW DOES YOUR BODY FEEL?

Take this moment to notice ourselves. Are we breathing? Notice if our bodies need to stretch, take a break, or get some fresh air. This accountability tool also serves to help us take care of ourselves. When needed, document exactly what you noticed from this moment and throughout this week. This will be useful to track stressors and triggers, which can be barriers to action steps.

☆ SELF CARE CHECKLIST

- ☐ Take 10 Deep Breaths
- ☐ Move! (Walk, Yoga, Run, Strut)
- ☐ Listen to Your Favorite Music
- ☐ Aromatherapy Time-Out
- ☐ Indulge in a Favorite __________
- ☐ Scream Out Loud!
- ☐ __________________

- ☐ __________________
- ☐ __________________
- ☐ __________________
- ☐ __________________
- ☐ __________________
- ☐ __________________
- ☐ __________________

I AM...

FREE WRITE PAGE

THE POWER OF PATTERNS

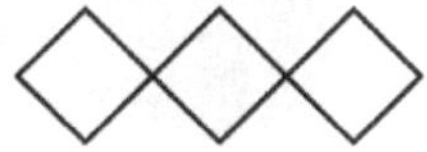

Let's practice noticing the factors within our life routine that harms our ability to feel happy and well.

When we know ourselves and have control over our own thoughts and bodies, we have the power to adjust ourselves and our routines.

Emotions are like waves. They come and go, alternating in urgency and strength. They have a beginning, a middle, and an end. They can come on gradually, sneaking up on us like a sudden and dangerously overwhelming high tide with a strange intensity, and then disappear as if they were never there in the first place. They can be influenced by the external, like the environment, seasons, or the people around us. Emotions, like waves, are never constant. They ebb and flow...always in motion. Always temporary. Never permanent. When we know they have a limited cycle and won't necessarily be the same the next day, or even the next hour, we can remind ourselves to relax into it and keep swimming so that we can survive and reach the surface. No matter how intense or powerful, we can assure ourselves that we only have to hold our breath for a moment longer and roll with it...keeping calm.

And when it has passed, we will have gotten through to the moment where it all simply dissolves into stillness. And we will know then that we can handle each wave as it comes, because they always disappear in the end.

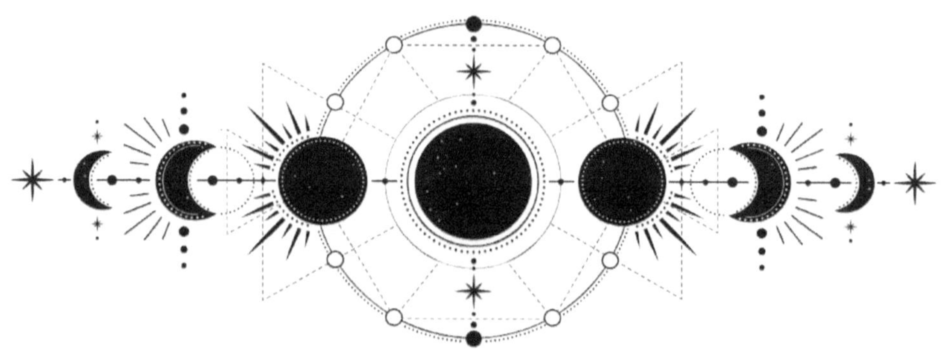

DATE:

SUNDAY

MONDAY

TUESDAY

WEDNESDAY

THURSDAY

FRIDAY

SATURDAY

THIS WEEK I AM MANIFESTING...

ACTION STEPS

What will be done by the end of the week?

TIMELINE   By when? (Day/Month)

RESPONSIBILITIES

Who will complete the prioritized tasks?

RESOURCES

(A) Resources Available (B) Resources Needed

COMMUNICATION PLAN

Who/What/When/Where/How
was it communicated?

POTENTIAL BARRIERS

What might cause resistance
to the ACTION STEPS? How?

GO GET IT MANTRA...

Choose a useful quote, image, or statement to serve as mental motivation. We must be loving of self when we choose this mantra.

GOAL OF THIS MOMENT

 TASK LIST

Write down 10 action items that will lead you to your goal.

ACCOMPLISHMENTS

Be loud, proud, and bold about the things we have been able to conquer this week. Cheer this moment, do a happy dance, and notice the tasks left behind, for they were always meant for next week's accomplishment section instead. Celebrate even the tiniest success and we will attract more.

HOW DOES YOUR BODY FEEL?

Take this moment to notice ourselves. Are we breathing? Notice if our bodies need to stretch, take a break, or get some fresh air. This accountability tool also serves to help us take care of ourselves. When needed, document exactly what you noticed from this moment and throughout this week. This will be useful to track stressors and triggers, which can be barriers to action steps.

⊛ SELF CARE CHECKLIST

☐ Take 10 Deep Breaths	☐ ______________________
☐ Move! (Walk, Yoga, Run, Strut)	☐ ______________________
☐ Listen to Your Favorite Music	☐ ______________________
☐ Aromatherapy Time-Out	☐ ______________________
☐ Indulge in a Favorite __________	☐ ______________________
☐ Scream Out Loud!	☐ ______________________
☐ ______________________	☐ ______________________

I AM...

FREE WRITE PAGE

Week 7

 MANIFESTATION WHEN
WE LOOK FOR IT

Practice visualizing success, noticing opportunities, and identifying lessons from failures. Implement strategies to find your tribe, because shared energy nurtures collective excellence.

Manifestation, when we look for it, reminds us of the power of positive thinking and intentional action in creating the life we want. One activity that can help us to manifest our desires is practicing visualization.

ACTIVITY

Set aside some time each day to visualize yourself achieving your goals and desires. Sit or lie down in a quiet place and close your eyes. Imagine yourself already in possession of what you desire, whether it's a new job, a relationship, or improved health. Visualize yourself feeling confident, happy, and fulfilled. Notice the details of your surroundings, the feelings in your body, and the sounds around you. As you visualize, allow yourself to feel a sense of gratitude for the abundance in your life.

Practicing visualization can help to train our minds to focus on positive outcomes and attract opportunities for success. By noticing opportunities and identifying lessons from failures, we can learn and grow from our experiences, rather than getting stuck in negative thought patterns. Finally, finding your tribe can also help to nurture collective excellence and support you on your journey toward manifestation.

Remember that manifestation is a process that requires patience, dedication, and consistent effort. Keep your focus on the positive outcomes you desire, and take intentional action toward them. With time and practice, you can become a powerful manifestor and create the life you truly want.

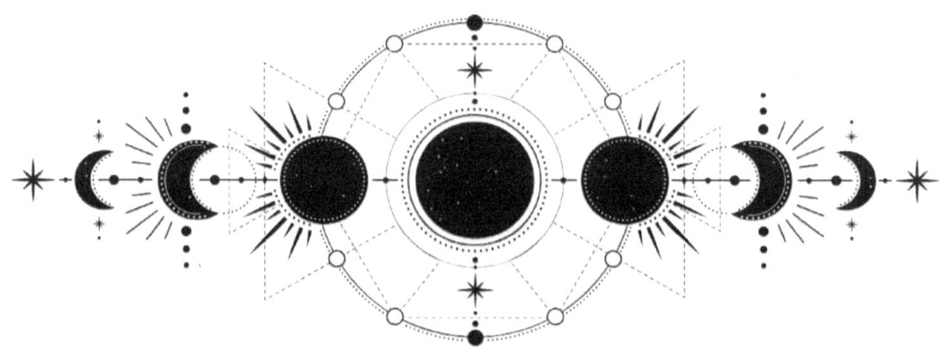

DATE:

SUNDAY
MONDAY
TUESDAY
WEDNESDAY
THURSDAY
FRIDAY
SATURDAY

THIS WEEK I AM MANIFESTING...

ACTION STEPS

What will be done by the end of the week?

TIMELINE   By when? (Day/Month)

RESPONSIBILITIES

Who will complete the prioritized tasks?

RESOURCES

(A) Resources Available (B) Resources Needed

COMMUNICATION PLAN

Who/What/When/Where/How was it communicated?

POTENTIAL BARRIERS

What might cause resistance to the ACTION STEPS? How?

GO GET IT MANTRA...

Choose a useful quote, image, or statement to serve as mental motivation. We must be loving of self when we choose this mantra.

GOAL OF THIS MOMENT

 TASK LIST

Write down 10 action items that will lead you to your goal.

ACCOMPLISHMENTS

Be loud, proud, and bold about the things we have been able to conquer this week. Cheer this moment, do a happy dance, and notice the tasks left behind, for they were always meant for next week's accomplishment section instead. Celebrate even the tiniest success and we will attract more.

HOW DOES YOUR BODY FEEL?

Take this moment to notice ourselves. Are we breathing? Notice if our bodies need to stretch, take a break, or get some fresh air. This accountability tool also serves to help us take care of ourselves. When needed, document exactly what you noticed from this moment and throughout this week. This will be useful to track stressors and triggers, which can be barriers to action steps.

⊛ SELF CARE CHECKLIST

☐ Take 10 Deep Breaths	☐ _______________
☐ Move! (Walk, Yoga, Run, Strut)	☐ _______________
☐ Listen to Your Favorite Music	☐ _______________
☐ Aromatherapy Time-Out	☐ _______________
☐ Indulge in a Favorite _________	☐ _______________
☐ Scream Out Loud!	☐ _______________
☐ _______________	☐ _______________

I AM...

FREE WRITE PAGE

Week 8

WRITTEN DOWN DREAMS
BECOME GOALS FULFILLED

"Written down dreams become goals fulfilled" is a powerful reminder of the importance of setting clear intentions and taking action toward our goals. One activity that can help us to turn our dreams into reality is journaling.

ACTIVITY

Set aside some time each day to journal about your dreams and goals. Begin by writing down your biggest dreams and desires, without judgment or self-editing. Then, break them down into smaller, achievable goals. Write down the steps you'll need to take to achieve each goal, and set deadlines for yourself. As you write, allow yourself to dream big and get excited about the possibilities.

Using journaling and therapeutic narratives can help us to clarify our desires, identify potential obstacles, and create a plan for achieving our goals. By breaking down our dreams into smaller, achievable goals, we can take action toward them in a more manageable way, building momentum and staying motivated. Remember to review your journal regularly and celebrate your progress along the way. With dedication, perseverance, and a clear vision, you can turn your dreams into reality.

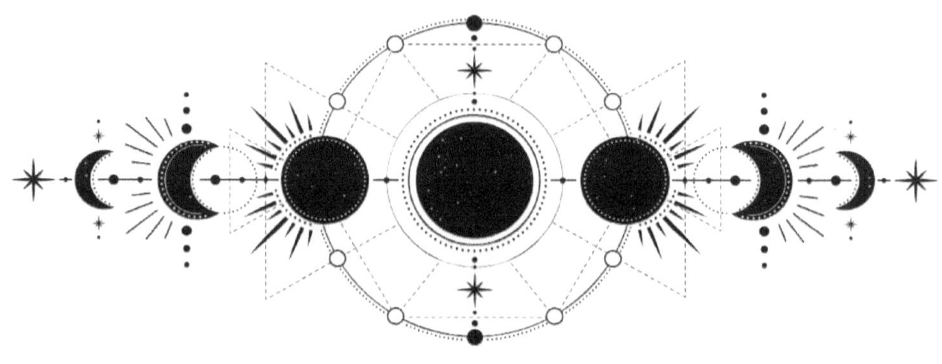

DATE:

SUNDAY
MONDAY
TUESDAY
WEDNESDAY
THURSDAY
FRIDAY
SATURDAY

THIS WEEK I AM MANIFESTING...

ACTION STEPS

What will be done by the end of the week?

TIMELINE   By when? (Day/Month)

RESPONSIBILITIES

Who will complete the prioritized tasks?

RESOURCES

(A) Resources Available (B) Resources Needed

COMMUNICATION PLAN

Who/What/When/Where/How
was it communicated?

POTENTIAL BARRIERS

What might cause resistance
to the ACTION STEPS? How?

GO GET IT MANTRA...

Choose a useful quote, image, or statement to serve as mental motivation. We must be loving of self when we choose this mantra.

GOAL OF THIS MOMENT

TASK LIST

Write down 10 action items that will lead you to your goal.

ACCOMPLISHMENTS

Be loud, proud, and bold about the things we have been able to conquer this week. Cheer this moment, do a happy dance, and notice the tasks left behind, for they were always meant for next week's accomplishment section instead. Celebrate even the tiniest success and we will attract more.

HOW DOES YOUR BODY FEEL?

Take this moment to notice ourselves. Are we breathing? Notice if our bodies need to stretch, take a break, or get some fresh air. This accountability tool also serves to help us take care of ourselves. When needed, document exactly what you noticed from this moment and throughout this week. This will be useful to track stressors and triggers, which can be barriers to action steps.

51 | Manifest it!

SELF CARE CHECKLIST

- [ ] Take 10 Deep Breaths
- [ ] Move! (Walk, Yoga, Run, Strut)
- [ ] Listen to Your Favorite Music
- [ ] Aromatherapy Time-Out
- [ ] Indulge in a Favorite __________
- [ ] Scream Out Loud!
- [ ] __________________

- [ ] __________________
- [ ] __________________
- [ ] __________________
- [ ] __________________
- [ ] __________________
- [ ] __________________
- [ ] __________________

I AM...

FREE WRITE PAGE

Week 9

WHAT'S YOUR ARCHETYPE?

A character archetype is a type of character who represents a universal pattern, and therefore appeals to our human "collective unconscious." Knowing about the archetypes gives you the opportunity to deepen your understanding of yourself and your motivations and set goals that align with your personal strengths and values.

First, read about different archetypes and what they represent.

(deksia.com/blog/strategy/brand-archetypes)

Next, explore the strengths and weaknesses of your archetype. Reflect on the strengths and weaknesses associated with it. Write down how these qualities show up in your life and relationships. How could they leverage their strengths and work on improving their weaknesses?

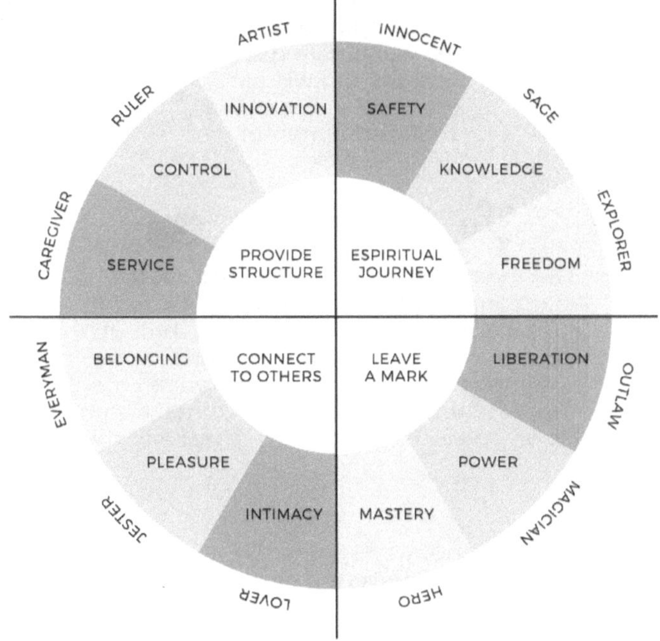

The Innocent
Exhibits happiness, goodness, optimism, safety, romance, and youth.

The Explorer
Finds inspiration in travel, risk, discovery, and the thrill of new experiences.

The Hero
On a mission to make the world a better place, the Hero is courageous, bold, and inspirational.

The Rebel
Questions authority and breaks the rules; the Rebel craves rebellion and revolution.

The Caregiver
Protects and cares for others, is compassionate, nurturing, and generous.

The Lover
Creates intimate moments, inspires love, passion, romance and commitment.

The Creator
Imaginative, inventive, and driven to build things of enduring meaning and value.

The Ruler
Creates order from the chaos; the Ruler is typically controlling and stern, yet responsible and organized.

The Sage
Committed to helping the world gain deeper insight and wisdom, the Sage serves as the thoughtful mentor or advisor.

The Magician
Wishes to create something special and make dreams a reality. The Magician is seen as visionary and spiritual.

The Everyman
Seeks connections and belonging; is recognized as supportive, faithful, and down-to-earth.

The Jester
Brings joy to the world through humor, fun, and irreverence. Often likes to make some mischief.

Enos, S. (2022, July 21). Brand archetypes:. DEKSIA.
https://deksia.com/blog/strategy/brand-archetypes

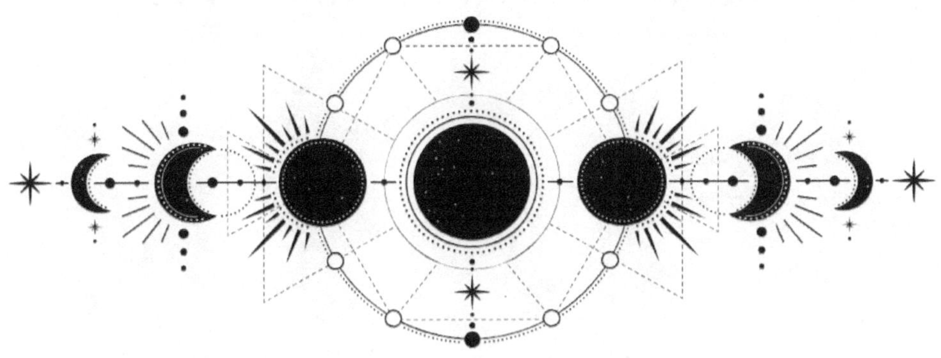

SUNDAY
MONDAY
TUESDAY
WEDNESDAY
THURSDAY
FRIDAY
SATURDAY

THIS WEEK I AM MANIFESTING...

ACTION STEPS

What will be done by the end of the week?

TIMELINE   By when? (Day/Month)

RESPONSIBILITIES

Who will complete the prioritized tasks?

RESOURCES

(A) Resources Available (B) Resources Needed

COMMUNICATION PLAN

Who/What/When/Where/How was it communicated?

POTENTIAL BARRIERS

What might cause resistance to the ACTION STEPS? How?

GO GET IT MANTRA...

Choose a useful quote, image, or statement to serve as mental motivation. We must be loving of self when we choose this mantra.

GOAL OF THIS MOMENT

TASK LIST

Write down 10 action items that will lead you to your goal.

ACCOMPLISHMENTS

Be loud, proud, and bold about the things we have been able to conquer this week. Cheer this moment, do a happy dance, and notice the tasks left behind, for they were always meant for next week's accomplishment section instead. Celebrate even the tiniest success and we will attract more.

HOW DOES YOUR BODY FEEL?

Take this moment to notice ourselves. Are we breathing? Notice if our bodies need to stretch, take a break, or get some fresh air. This accountability tool also serves to help us take care of ourselves. When needed, document exactly what you noticed from this moment and throughout this week. This will be useful to track stressors and triggers, which can be barriers to action steps.

⊛ SELF CARE CHECKLIST

- ☐ Take 10 Deep Breaths
- ☐ Move! (Walk, Yoga, Run, Strut)
- ☐ Listen to Your Favorite Music
- ☐ Aromatherapy Time-Out
- ☐ Indulge in a Favorite _________
- ☐ Scream Out Loud!
- ☐ _____________________

- ☐ _____________________
- ☐ _____________________
- ☐ _____________________
- ☐ _____________________
- ☐ _____________________
- ☐ _____________________
- ☐ _____________________

I AM...

FREE WRITE PAGE

Week 10

SELF- AWARENESS LEADS TO EMPOWERMENT: THE BRAIN WELL-BEING MODEL

Self- awareness and insight building refers to the practice of being aware of our feelings, emotions, body sensations, and relationships with self and others. With appropriate insight comes the ability to be compassionate towards ourselves and others. It involves developing the essential components of well-being such as aspirational awareness, perceptual awareness, relational awareness, and somatic awareness. By practicing compassionate systems awareness, we can improve our mental health and overall well-being through habitual practices that empower our best selves.

Learning to "walk in someone else's shoes", provides an opportunity to be a witness and observer. It cultivates compassion as we try to understand and empathize with the person and complex intersecting greater systems/forces at play in their lives and communities. Cultivating compassion is vital in everyday human interactions as it aligns our thoughts, affects how we think and feel, and influences our behavior with regards to how we act and connect with those around us.

Without compassion, we react to situations that seem out of our control and place blame on others without taking accountability for how our actions played a role in those circumstances/outcomes we are facing. With compassion, we become better humans by caring for one another and feel a greater connection to other humans and the world. When we feel connected to others and our world, we treat ourselves and our fellow man better.

This week we practice compassion through reflection and mindfulness.

COMPASSION JOURNALISM

Take some time each day to reflect on moments when you showed compassion towards others, as well as times when you could have responded with more compassion. Write down your thoughts and feelings, and brainstorm ways in which you can cultivate more compassion in your daily life. With a clear vision, you can turn your dreams into reality.

BRAIN WELL-BEING MODEL

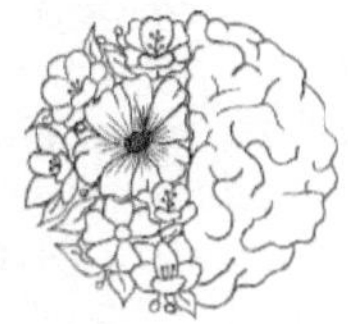

Compassionate Systems Awareness, developed by Peter Senge and Mette Boell, merges a way of thinking that involves developing an improved understanding of the world through focusing on the relationships and interactions among its components. This approach promotes a holistic understanding of systems that prioritizes interconnectedness, empathy, collaboration, resilience, and collective well-being.

The Brain Well-Being Model furthers the story of interconnectedness by emphasizing the vital role of self-awareness and social connection to our well-being. Our brains, honed over millennia in social groups, inherently crave connection for optimal functioning. This craving is rooted in several key factors:

- Social support reduces stress by activating neural pathways that promote feelings of relaxation and safety,
- Positive social interactions reinforce neural circuits associated with joy, trust, and contentment, enhancing our emotional resilience.
- Feeling secure in connection with others fosters the development of empathy and social cognition skills, essential for navigating complex social dynamics,
- The release of oxytocin and dopamine during social interactions reinforces bonding and rewards, further promoting well-being. Recognizing this intrinsic need for connection underscores the critical importance of social relationships for mental health and overall flourishing.

This *Brain Well-Being Model* fosters social-emotional learning that cultivates insight into how to improve well-being in self and others. Here's how:

- **Emotional Intelligence:** By connecting somatic sensations with emotions, somatic awareness, we gain insight into our emotional states and develop healthy coping mechanisms. When we can make better sense of how our bodies react when we are engaged in a behavior or experience that causes physical discomfort; we can have better insight into the choices we can make to avoid the discomfort we notice in the future.

- **Empathy and Relationships:** Exploring relational awareness fosters empathy and interpersonal skills, crucial for navigating social dynamics and building healthy connections across cultures. When we feel disconnected, alone and unsafe, it can decrease our emotional intelligence, lessen trust in our ability to be a part of a connected system, and increase belief in faulty, unproven and unhealthy thoughts because we haven't been able to process in writing or talk about them; which would have provided a chance to prove the thoughts wrong.

- **Cognitive Restructuring:** Focusing on *perceptual awareness* allows us to challenge negative thought patterns and develop resilience through self-reflection. Storytelling empowers and to be heard is to heal. When we keep a story on replay on the big internal screen of images filtering through our brains; it's best to choose the story that by its end...causes us to smile. The story we believe about ourselves is the one that others believe too. This impacts opportunities and growth through the lifespan.

- **Goal-Setting and Motivation:** *Aspirational awareness* empowers us to set goals aligned with our values, fostering a sense of purpose and growth. Seeing ourselves as powerful and able is the way toward being powerful and able. Written down dreams become goals fulfilled. We must think about what having our goal achieved might look like for us so that we can consistently make decisions and take actions that get us closer to the vision we see of ourselves. Never seen anyone do what you wanted to do that has your same experience of life? When you do it, make sure to share so that you can change that reality for someone else. Think It. Write It. Will It. Do it. Claim it... and take pictures.

- **Community Building:** Through interactive prompts and insight-building activities, the *Brain Well-Being Model* can offer learning and connection that promotes a sense of community and belonging through self-accountability. We are held accountable to know that we need connection to each other because the brain needs socialization and when human beings are isolated from each other for too long, it becomes an extreme barrier to their wellness. We must engage in *Collective Care* where we care for self, care for others, and never stop until we are all cared for because our world's well-being depends upon it.

In Summary, the *Brain Well-Being Model* encourages us to explore connections not just in isolation, but within the context of these four awarenesses. This holistic approach allows us to see how our **somatic sensations** might influence our **perceptions**, which in turn might impact our **aspirations** and the quality of our **relationships**. By using this newfound knowledge, we can build healthier routines that support our overall well-being and propel us towards a more fulfilling life that aligns with our deepest desires.

BRAIN WELL-BEING MODEL

Listed below are prompts to spark self-exploration across different aspects of self as we take actionable steps toward empowering brain well-being.

SOMATIC AWARENESS

What is my body telling me?

ASPIRATIONAL AWARENESS

What is my purpose?

PERCEPTUAL AWARENESS

What are the stories I am telling myself?

RELATIONAL AWARENESS

How am I connected with others?

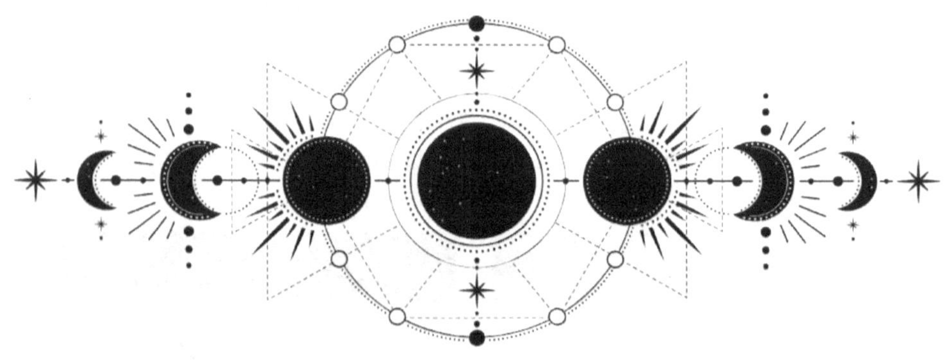

DATE:

SUNDAY

MONDAY

TUESDAY

WEDNESDAY

THURSDAY

FRIDAY

SATURDAY

THIS WEEK I AM MANIFESTING...

ACTION STEPS

What will be done by the end of the week?

TIMELINE   By when? (Day/Month)

RESPONSIBILITIES

Who will complete the prioritized tasks?

RESOURCES

(A) Resources Available (B) Resources Needed

COMMUNICATION PLAN

Who/What/When/Where/How was it communicated?

POTENTIAL BARRIERS

What might cause resistance to the ACTION STEPS? How?

GO GET IT MANTRA...

Choose a useful quote, image, or statement to serve as mental motivation. We must be loving of self when we choose this mantra.

GOAL OF THIS MOMENT

 TASK LIST

Write down 10 action items that will lead you to your goal.

ACCOMPLISHMENTS

Be loud, proud, and bold about the things we have been able to conquer this week. Cheer this moment, do a happy dance, and notice the tasks left behind, for they were always meant for next week's accomplishment section instead. Celebrate even the tiniest success and we will attract more.

HOW DOES YOUR BODY FEEL?

Take this moment to notice ourselves. Are we breathing? Notice if our bodies need to stretch, take a break, or get some fresh air. This accountability tool also serves to help us take care of ourselves. When needed, document exactly what you noticed from this moment and throughout this week. This will be useful to track stressors and triggers, which can be barriers to action steps.

⊛ SELF CARE CHECKLIST

☐ Take 10 Deep Breaths

☐ Move! (Walk, Yoga, Run, Strut)

☐ Listen to Your Favorite Music

☐ Aromatherapy Time-Out

☐ Indulge in a Favorite __________

☐ Scream Out Loud!

☐ __________________

☐ __________________

☐ __________________

☐ __________________

☐ __________________

☐ __________________

☐ __________________

☐ __________________

I AM...

FREE WRITE PAGE

Week 11

SOMATIC AWARENESS LEADS TO PEACE

Somatic awareness is the art of listening to the silent language of our bodies. It transcends the realm of physical presence, inviting us to delve into the intricate symphony of sensations, signals, and subtle cues that our bodies constantly offer. Imagine our bodies are wise companions, speaking to us in whispers that convey its needs, emotions, and responses to the world around us. It's whispering secrets from our bodies to our minds keep us safe and protected. Forget just knowing we have a body – this is about understanding its unique language: the tingles, the tightness, the rumblings. It's like our bodies are constantly trying to talk to us, and somatic awareness is the key to deciphering its messages.

We're talking way beyond "am I comfy?" This is about what that tightness in our chest or the butterflies in our stomachs are really trying to tell us. Maybe it's anxiety whispering, or maybe it's just our bodies' way of saying "hey, chill out!" The coolest part? Our bodies don't exist in a vacuum. What we're thinking, feeling, even the weather outside – all of it can influence how we feel physically. The people we are around can also influence how our bodies react. By tuning into this internal conversation, we unlock a deeper understanding of ourselves. With improved Somatic Awareness, we can manage our emotions better, stress less, and feel more connected to ourselves as a whole person – mind, body, and spirit!

At its essence, somatic awareness encourages us to perceive our body as more than just a vessel, but as a dynamic entity with its own vocabulary of sensations and signals. It entails being attuned to the nuances of bodily experiences beyond basic sensory perceptions, recognizing the profound significance of each twitch, tingle, and ache. By developing somatic awareness, we embark on a journey of self-discovery and introspection, unlocking the profound wisdom encoded within our physical forms. This heightened sensitivity fosters a deeper connection to our emotions, thoughts, and surroundings, empowering us to navigate life with greater mindfulness, resilience, and authenticity.

THE RELATIONSHIP BETWEEN MENTAL AND PHYSICAL HEALTH

The relationship between mental and physical health is closely interconnected. Our mental health can have a significant impact on our physical health, and vice versa. Optimal physical health requires somatic awareness, which is being in tune with our bodies and regulating our nervous system to better manage big emotions. The body remembers and recognizes environments or situations that have triggered a stress response in the past and if we learn to listen to it, we can be empowered.

When we are able to be present with how our body reacts when we are stressed or overwhelmed, we can take power from a situation by engaging in coping strategies before the stress response even hits us. Our coping strategies then work to delay or completely avoid the maladaptive stress response we normally engage in.

One activity that can help to improve both mental and physical health is dancing. Dancing builds our somatic awareness by helping us to create a safe space for our bodies and energy through movement.

ACTIVITY

Put on some music that makes you feel good and start dancing! Let yourself move freely, without judgment or self-consciousness. Focus on the physical sensations in your body as you move, and let go of any stress or tension. Dancing can help to improve cardiovascular health, flexibility, and coordination, while also boosting mood and reducing stress.

By engaging in regular physical activity like dancing, we can also use it for socialization and relationship building by breathing with and connecting to other people with shared experiences as humans. Exercise releases endorphins, which are natural mood-boosters, while also promoting relaxation and reducing stress. Additionally, moving our bodies can help us to connect with our thoughts about our emotions and help us to release emotional tension that may be impacting our mental health.

Remember to choose an activity that incorporates your body and movement and breath that you enjoy.

Don't forget to have fun with it!

SOMATIC AWARENESS

The Body Keeps Score: The body also remembers all the physical and emotional stress/trauma.

Developing Bodily Awareness

Through various meditation techniques, such as Grounding, Resourcing & Visualization, Body Scans, and being in sunshine, we can help regulate our nervous system, especially the vagus nerve.

Building the Foundation to Improve Yourself

Remove mental, emotional & physical blocks that prevent us from being our best self. Notice how the body is feeling when feeling bad or good so that we can make better choices.

Treating Symptoms Effectively

Once we know there is an issue, we can treat a range of conditions such as PTSD, Anxiety, Depression, Chronic Pain & Substance Use Disorders.

The vagus nerve represents the parasympathetic nervous system, which oversees a vast array of crucial bodily functions, including control of mood, immune response, digestion, and heart rate.

Transforming & Releasing Trauma

With a practice of awareness, we begin to address triggers & trauma stored in the body. We do this with mindful exercises such as yoga, which helps decrease blockages in the nervous system.

Releasing Tension

Reset & recondition the nervous system back to a balanced state. Breathing and getting enough rest and healthy food is a big part in helping the body know it's time to relax.

SOMATIC AWARENESS EXERCISES

GROUNDING

Move the body
Move in ways that feel the most comfortable. While moving, focus on how the body feels - one body part at a time. Inhale and exhale with intention while moving.

Focus on the breath
Begin by slowly inhaling through the nose for four seconds, then exhale from the mouth for three seconds. Continue with this breathing pattern and repeat positive affirmations to yourself. Practice this for at least three minutes.

Tense and relax different muscles
Become aware of the physical body - start by pressing the feet into the ground as hard as you can for a few seconds. Release the pressure and notice how the feet feel. Practice this exercise with various body parts.

RESOURCING AND VISUALIZATION

Create a safe place in the mind
Go back to a time that felt safe and happy or think of a new place that would reflect these same feelings. Think about the smell, texture, and colors. Feel the body there and focus on any feelings that arise.

Think about those who bring feelings of peace
Look at photos of them or visualize specific memories. Participate in an activity that reminds you of them.

BODY SCANS

Cultivating mindfulness Body Scan meditation
1. Bring awareness to the body by taking a few deep breaths. Take note of any present feelings or sensations.
2. As you inhale, invite in expansion. As you exhale, invite in relaxation.
3. Notice if there's any pressure on the legs and arms. Notice if the body is holding onto any tension. Clench fists, release fists...exhaling with the release.
4. Relax the jaw and face muscles.
5. Wiggle fingers/toes. Breathing in & out, slowly come back into stillness.

All these exercises are a great way to relieve stress and anxiety. They can be performed sitting, lying down, or in other postures. Each exercise can be practiced together or on its own.

SOMATIC AWARENESS AFFIRMATIONS

Crown Chakra *I know/I understand...*
Third Eye Chakra *I see...*
Throat Chakra *I speak/I love...*
Heart Chakra *I care/I feel...*
Solar Plexus *I am...*
Sacrum/Sacral Chakra *I want...*
Root Chakra *I need...*

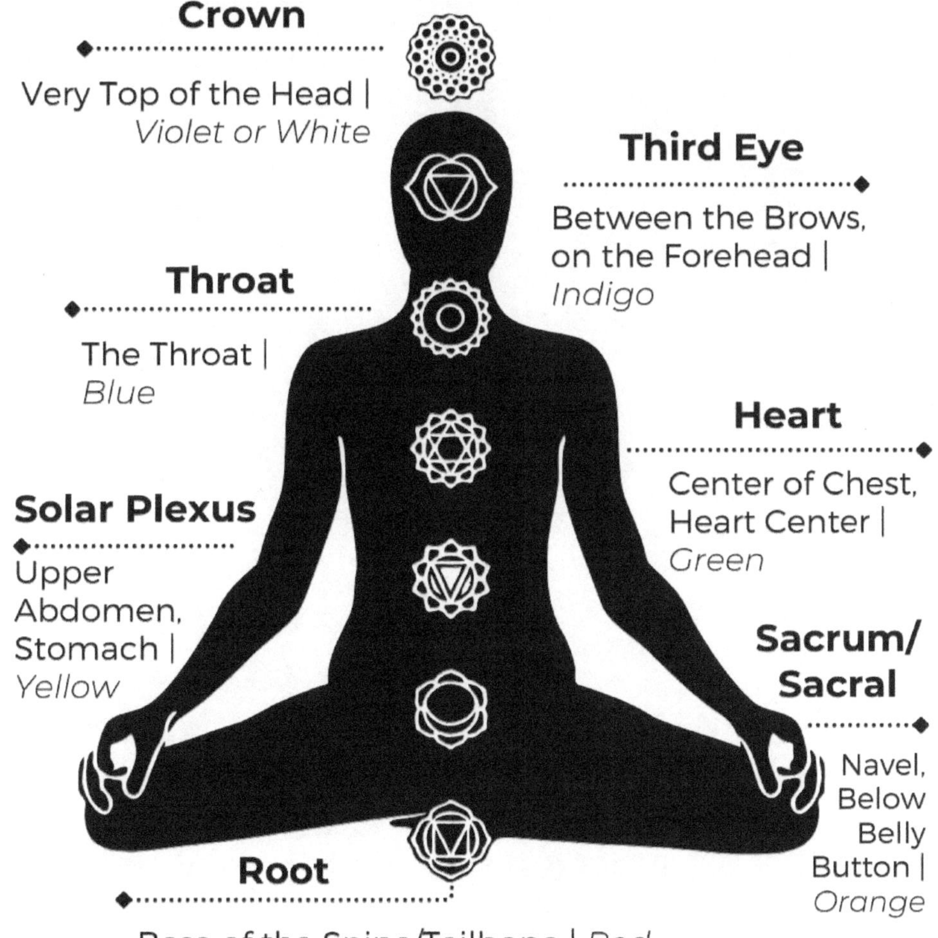

THE FEELING WHEEL

This week, review the feeling wheel and think about how some of those feelings might be showing up in your body. Explore for yourself, through written words, how you may release some of those feelings from your body and let them go.

The Feeling Wheel was designed by Gloria Willcox (1982) and is a great starting point for those who find it challenging to identify their emotions.

You can use the wheel to explore the emotions you are feeling at any given moment of the day.

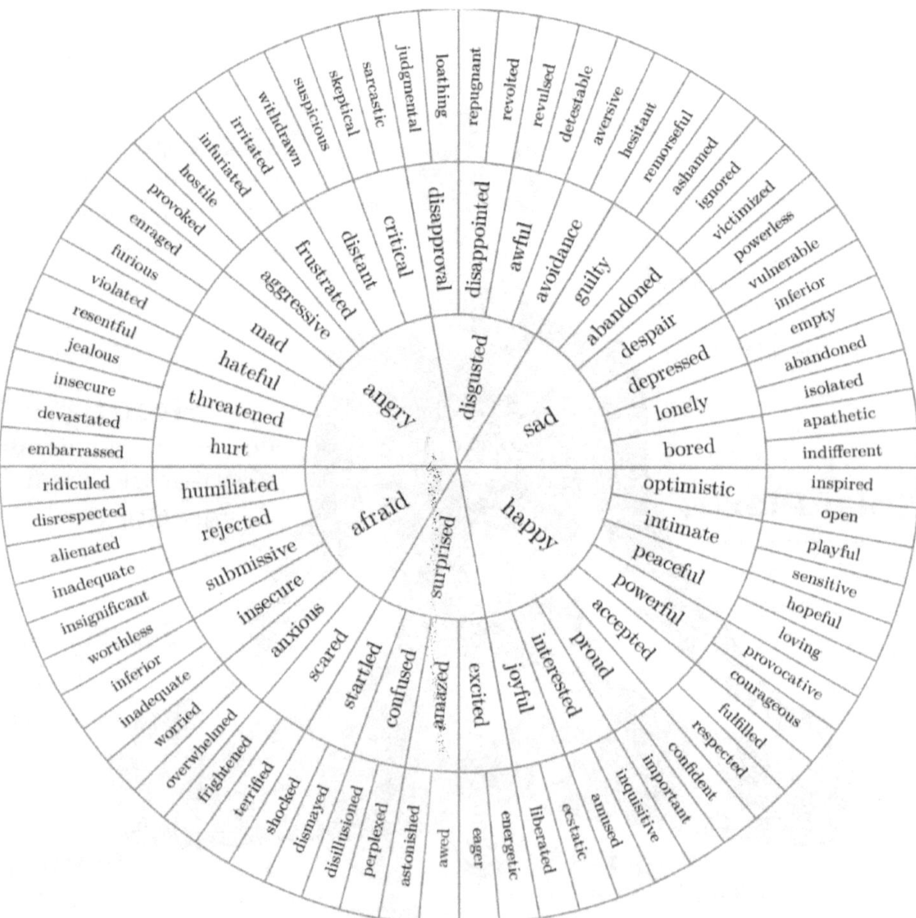

The feeling wheel: A tool for expanding awareness of emotions and ... (n.d.). https://journals.sagepub.com/doi/abs/10.1177/036215378201200411

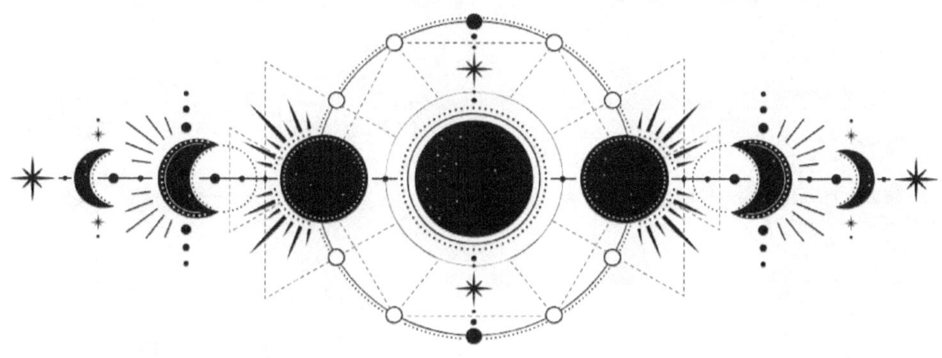

SUNDAY
MONDAY
TUESDAY
WEDNESDAY
THURSDAY
FRIDAY
SATURDAY

THIS WEEK I AM MANIFESTING...

ACTION STEPS

What will be done by the end of the week?

TIMELINE   By when? (Day/Month)

RESPONSIBILITIES

Who will complete the prioritized tasks?

RESOURCES

(A) Resources Available (B) Resources Needed

COMMUNICATION PLAN

Who/What/When/Where/How was it communicated?

POTENTIAL BARRIERS

What might cause resistance to the ACTION STEPS? How?

GO GET IT MANTRA...

Choose a useful quote, image, or statement to serve as mental motivation. We must be loving of self when we choose this mantra.

GOAL OF THIS MOMENT

⊛ TASK LIST

Write down 10 action items that will lead you to your goal.

ACCOMPLISHMENTS

Be loud, proud, and bold about the things we have been able to conquer this week. Cheer this moment, do a happy dance, and notice the tasks left behind, for they were always meant for next week's accomplishment section instead. Celebrate even the tiniest success and we will attract more.

HOW DOES YOUR BODY FEEL?

Take this moment to notice ourselves. Are we breathing? Notice if our bodies need to stretch, take a break, or get some fresh air. This accountability tool also serves to help us take care of ourselves. When needed, document exactly what you noticed from this moment and throughout this week. This will be useful to track stressors and triggers, which can be barriers to action steps.

⊛ SELF CARE CHECKLIST

- ☐ Take 10 Deep Breaths
- ☐ Move! (Walk, Yoga, Run, Strut)
- ☐ Listen to Your Favorite Music
- ☐ Aromatherapy Time-Out
- ☐ Indulge in a Favorite ___________
- ☐ Scream Out Loud!
- ☐ ___________

- ☐ ___________
- ☐ ___________
- ☐ ___________
- ☐ ___________
- ☐ ___________
- ☐ ___________
- ☐ ___________

I AM...

FREE WRITE PAGE

Week 12

ASPIRATIONAL AWARENESS LEADS TO PURPOSE

Aspirational awareness intentionally focuses on identifying and pursuing one's aspirations and goals. It involves becoming aware of our purpose, goals, and intentions for how we want to show up in the world. It involves developing a clear understanding of what we want to achieve in life and taking intentional action toward those goals.

Aspirational awareness is important because it provides direction and purpose to our lives and helps us to prioritize our time and energy towards activities that align with our goals. By practicing aspirational awareness, we gain clarity about our values and aspirations and can develop a positive mindset and outlook on life. Its benefits include increased motivation, focus, creativity, inspiration, and a sense of fulfillment as we progress toward our aspirations.

Affirmations can help strengthen self-worth by boosting our positive opinion of ourselves and confidence in our ability to achieve our goals. We can counter the feelings of panic, stress, and self-doubt that often accompany anxiety with positive self-talk.

Attainable aspirations require goal setting and awareness of where we are aiming our efforts toward. As we make choices and decisions in life, we must notice how our choices impact outcomes.

CREATE A VISION BOARD

Create a vision board that represents your aspirations and goals. This could be a physical board with pictures and words that inspire you or a digital board created using a tool like Pinterest. Display your vision board in a place where you will see it often, and use it as a source of motivation and inspiration.

UPLIFTING CULTURE: A LOOK AT...
INTERGENERATIONAL TRAUMA

GRANDPARENTS

- Oppression
- Domestic Violence,
- Abuse
- PTSD
- Patriarchy
- Chemical Dependency
- Extreme Poverty

PARENTS

- Alcoholism
- Physical Abuse
- Repressed Anger
- Emotional Abuse
- Untreated Mental Illness
- Codependency

YOU

- Approval Seeking
- Identity
- Confusion
- Eating Disorder
- Depression
- Anxiety
- Alcoholism
- Attachment Issues,
- Codependency

Home. BROWN GIRL TRAUMA. (2023, August 24).
https://browngirltrauma.com/

UPLIFTING CULTURE: A LOOK AT...
MOTIVATION OVER LAZINESS

Kaizen | *Making Small Improvements*
Kaizen refers to focusing on small improvements, every day, and aiming to become 1% better each day rather than striving for perfection from the outset.

Shinrin-Yoku | *The Art of Forest Bathing*
Shinrin-Yoku refers to the practice of spending time outdoors with nature. "Taking in the forest atmosphere is proven to lower heart rate, reduce stress, and improve your immune system." - Earl of East

Ikigai | *Your Reason for Being*
Ikigai means having a purpose; your reason for being. The 4 rules of ikigai: do what you love, do what you're good at, do what the world needs, do what you can be paid for.

Wabi Sabi | *Beauty in Imperfection*
The concept of wabi sabi is that rather than perfection, one should find beauty in imperfection. Forget the idea of flaws and faults, and embrace the imperfect details of your self, body, past, and present.

Shoshin | *A Beginner Mindset*
Shoshin is a concept from Zen Buddhism that involves approaching things with a beginner's mindset.

Hara Hachi Bu | *Satisfied, Not Full*
This technique is the practical concept of stopping eating when you're 80% full, rather than 100%.

Ganbaru | *Doing Your Best*
This means that one should be patient, do their absolute best, keep going through tough times, and accomplish goals.

Montano, C. F. (2017, April 2). A Japanese technique for overcoming laziness. Bright Side - Inspiration. Creativity. Wonder. https://brightside.me/articles/a-japanese-technique-for-overcoming-laziness-11255/

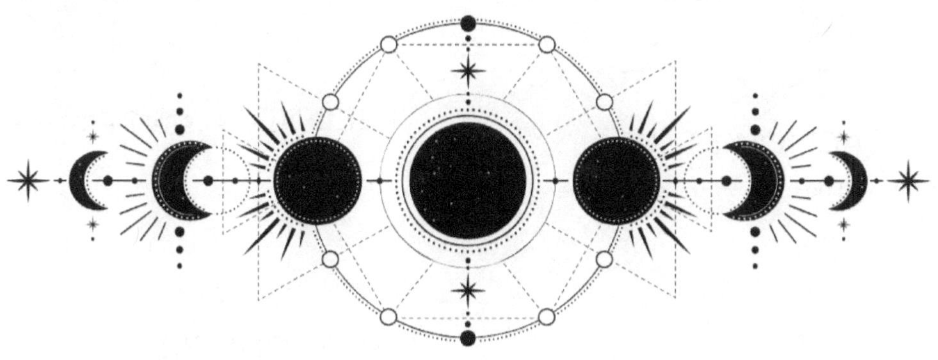

DATE:

| SUNDAY |
| MONDAY |
| TUESDAY |
| WEDNESDAY |
| THURSDAY |
| FRIDAY |
| SATURDAY |

THIS WEEK I AM MANIFESTING...

ACTION STEPS

What will be done by the end of the week?

TIMELINE   By when? (Day/Month)

RESPONSIBILITIES

Who will complete the prioritized tasks?

RESOURCES

(A) Resources Available (B) Resources Needed

COMMUNICATION PLAN

Who/What/When/Where/How was it communicated?

POTENTIAL BARRIERS

What might cause resistance to the ACTION STEPS? How?

GO GET IT MANTRA...

Choose a useful quote, image, or statement to serve as mental motivation. We must be loving of self when we choose this mantra.

GOAL OF THIS MOMENT

⊛ TASK LIST

Write down 10 action items that will lead you to your goal.

ACCOMPLISHMENTS

Be loud, proud, and bold about the things we have been able to conquer this week. Cheer this moment, do a happy dance, and notice the tasks left behind, for they were always meant for next week's accomplishment section instead. Celebrate even the tiniest success and we will attract more.

HOW DOES YOUR BODY FEEL?

Take this moment to notice ourselves. Are we breathing? Notice if our bodies need to stretch, take a break, or get some fresh air. This accountability tool also serves to help us take care of ourselves. When needed, document exactly what you noticed from this moment and throughout this week. This will be useful to track stressors and triggers, which can be barriers to action steps.

⊛ SELF CARE CHECKLIST

☐ Take 10 Deep Breaths	☐ ______________________
☐ Move! (Walk, Yoga, Run, Strut)	☐ ______________________
☐ Listen to Your Favorite Music	☐ ______________________
☐ Aromatherapy Time-Out	☐ ______________________
☐ Indulge in a Favorite __________	☐ ______________________
☐ Scream Out Loud!	☐ ______________________
☐ ______________________	☐ ______________________

I AM...

FREE WRITE PAGE

PERCEPTUAL AWARENESS LEAD TO GREATER INSIGHT

Perceptual awareness is the ability to be aware of the story you tell yourself about yourself, as well as the stories you tell others and the stories they believe and tell about you.

Perceptual awareness refers to the ability to perceive and interpret sensory information and experiences in a meaningful way. It involves being open to different perspectives and interpretations of reality and being able to adjust our mindset and beliefs in response to new information.

Perceptual awareness is important because it allows us to see things in a new light, gain a deeper understanding of ourselves and others, and develop a more open-minded and empathetic approach to life. By practicing perceptual awareness, we can enhance our communication skills, improve our relationships, and gain greater insight into our own biases and assumptions. Its benefits include increased empathy, creativity, innovation, problem-solving skills, and personal growth.

CHANGE YOUR PERSPECTIVE THIS WEEK

Choose a situation or problem that you've been struggling with and try to view it from a different perspective. This could involve imagining how someone else might approach the situation, or trying to see it through a new lens or mindset. Write down your new insights and observations. Reflect on how this exercise impacted your perception of the situation.

PERCEPTUAL AWARENESS THROUGH STORYTELLING

Storytelling connects us, helps us make sense of the world, and communicates our values and beliefs.

Self-Told

"The story we tell others about who we are."

Promotes *self-awareness* and a better understanding of our perception of the world by summarizing personal experiences to help others understand us.

What Other People Think

"The story others say about us."

Creates *empathy* and a better understanding of others by listening to how they engage in storytelling about us and themselves.

Actions Driven

"The story our actions tell."

Awareness of how action taken, or lack of *action* taken, in our lives can help us better define and control our own narrative.

The power of storytelling to facilitate human connection and learning. The Power of Storytelling to Facilitate Human Connection and Learning | IMPACT. (n.d.). https://sites.bu.edu/impact/previous-issues/impact-summer-2022/the-power-of-storytelling/

THE STORIES WE TELL...

- The story you're born into
- The story of what happened to you
- The story you tell yourself
- The story you tell others
- The story others tell about you
- The story your actions tell
- The story that will be told about you after you die

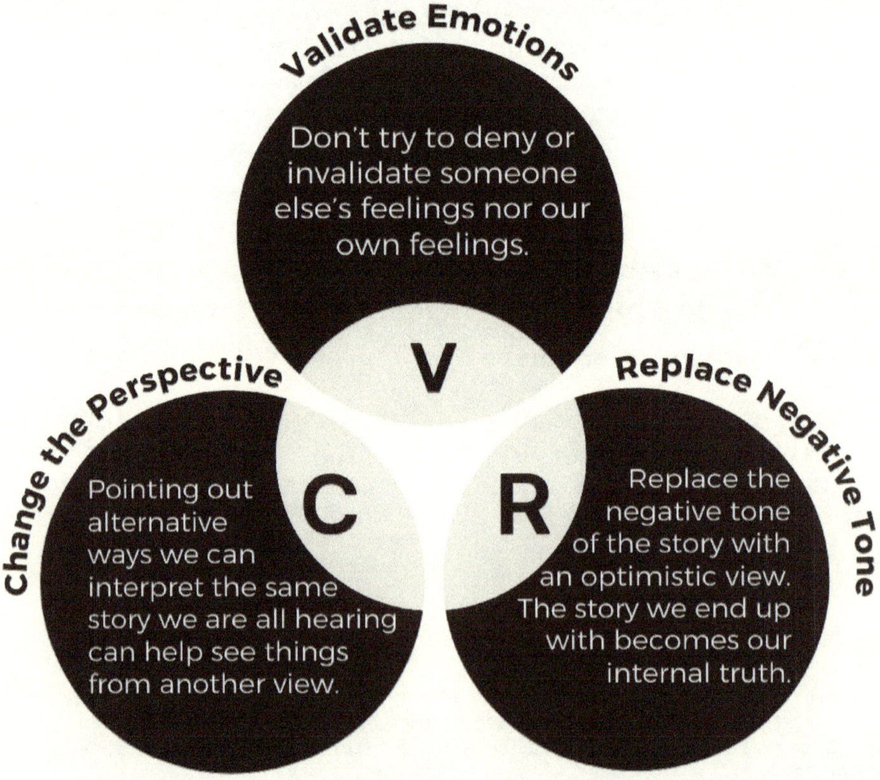

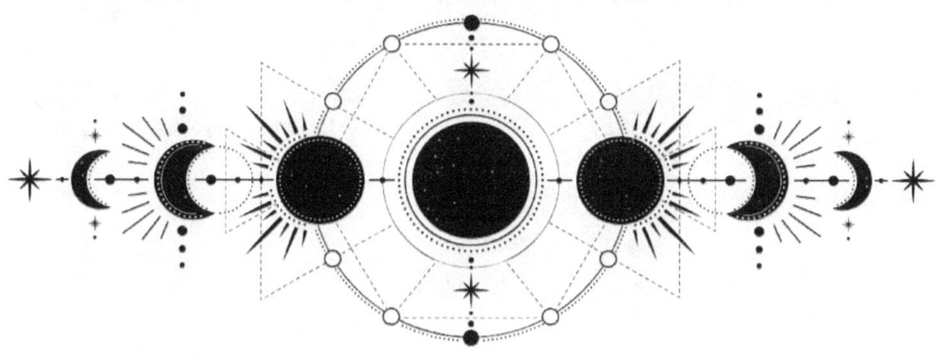

DATE:

SUNDAY
MONDAY
TUESDAY
WEDNESDAY
THURSDAY
FRIDAY
SATURDAY

THIS WEEK I AM MANIFESTING...

ACTION STEPS

What will be done by the end of the week?

TIMELINE   By when? (Day/Month)

RESPONSIBILITIES

Who will complete the prioritized tasks?

RESOURCES

(A) Resources Available (B) Resources Needed

COMMUNICATION PLAN

Who/What/When/Where/How was it communicated?

POTENTIAL BARRIERS

What might cause resistance to the ACTION STEPS? How?

GO GET IT MANTRA...

Choose a useful quote, image, or statement to serve as mental motivation. We must be loving of self when we choose this mantra.

GOAL OF THIS MOMENT

TASK LIST

Write down 10 action items that will lead you to your goal.

ACCOMPLISHMENTS

Be loud, proud, and bold about the things we have been able to conquer this week. Cheer this moment, do a happy dance, and notice the tasks left behind, for they were always meant for next week's accomplishment section instead. Celebrate even the tiniest success and we will attract more.

HOW DOES YOUR BODY FEEL?

Take this moment to notice ourselves. Are we breathing? Notice if our bodies need to stretch, take a break, or get some fresh air. This accountability tool also serves to help us take care of ourselves. When needed, document exactly what you noticed from this moment and throughout this week. This will be useful to track stressors and triggers, which can be barriers to action steps.

⊛ SELF CARE CHECKLIST

- ☐ Take 10 Deep Breaths
- ☐ Move! (Walk, Yoga, Run, Strut)
- ☐ Listen to Your Favorite Music
- ☐ Aromatherapy Time-Out
- ☐ Indulge in a Favorite __________
- ☐ Scream Out Loud!
- ☐ __________

- ☐ __________
- ☐ __________
- ☐ __________
- ☐ __________
- ☐ __________
- ☐ __________
- ☐ __________

I AM...

FREE WRITE PAGE

Week 14

RELATIONAL AWARENESS LEADS TO IMPROVED RELATIONSHIPS

Relational awareness refers to the ability to understand and navigate the dynamics of our interpersonal relationships. It involves being aware of our own emotions and behaviors, as well as those of others, and being able to communicate and connect with others in a healthy and meaningful way.

Relational awareness is important because it helps us to build and maintain strong, supportive relationships. It helps us navigate conflicts and challenges in a constructive way. By practicing relational awareness, we can enhance our communication skills, deepen our empathy and understanding of others, and build stronger, more fulfilling relationships. Its benefits include increased emotional intelligence, better conflict resolution skills, improved self-awareness, and enhanced well-being.

REFLECT ON YOUR RELATIONSHIPS

Take some time to reflect on your relationships with friends, family, coworkers, and acquaintances. Consider how you communicate with them, how you express your needs and boundaries, and how you respond to their needs and boundaries. Identify any areas where you could improve your communication or deepen your connection with others, and make a plan to take action.

SETTING BOUNDARIES

Boundaries are the limits, rules, or lines we set for our own personal comfort. Healthy boundaries define what is appropriate behavior in our relationships – behavior that keeps both parties safe. Setting healthy boundaries is crucial for self-care and positive relationships. Setting healthy boundaries requires self-awareness. We need to be clear about our expectations of ourselves and others, and what we are, and are not, comfortable with in specific situations.

Leaders in healthcare, such as Psychologist Richard Davidson, founder of The Center for Healthy Minds, propose that concepts such as awareness (somatic), connection (relational), insight (perceptual), and purpose (aspirational) are imperative to attaining optimal well-being because they assist us in noticing, in the moment, what makes our minds, bodies, and spirits feel well.

When we talk about "doing the work", in therapeutic or reflective treatments, participants are often encouraged to explore the modification of routines and/or relationships that seemingly cause us harm or hinder growth. Much of the work lies in setting boundaries as the first step toward an empowered mindset.

Setting healthy boundaries requires good communication skills that convey assertiveness and clarity. Manifesting works best when we are confident and safe and feeling able. Making powerfully productive choices by engaging in boundary setting is a healthy practice to engage in.

Setting boundaries gives us the disciplinary skills needed to help us make better choices. Communicating our boundaries with the people in our lives may help them to understand our limits and how we expect to be treated. In turn, they may take our boundaries into consideration and adjust their behavior or they may behave in ways that will inform our decisions about their roles in our lives.

BOUNDARIES
PHYSICAL
• Personal space
• Body
• Privacy
MATERIAL
• Giving or lending things
• Your financials
• Monetary decisions
EMOTIONAL
• Thoughts, feelings, values, beliefs
• How much are you willing to share?
TIME
• Limits on energy given to others
• How you manage your time
VERBAL
• How you allow others to talk to you
• What you feel is appropriate to discuss
SEXUAL
• Giving consent, sexual touch, intimacy and desires

(2019) Mette Miriam Böll, Peter Senge. Introduction to the Compassionate Systems Framework in Schools. Ackerman, Courtney E. (2023, June 3) What Is Self-Awareness? (+5 Ways to Be More Self-Aware). https://positivepsychology.com/self-awareness-matters-how-you-can-be-more-self-aware/

Duval & Wicklund, 1972 - Ackerman, Courtney E. (2023, June 3) What Is Self-Awareness? (+5 Ways to Be More Self-Aware). https://positivepsychology.com/self-awareness-matters-how-you-can-be-more-self-aware/

CASEL FRAMEWORK

The CASEL framework, developed by the Collaborative for Academic, Social, and Emotional Learning (CASEL), promotes social and emotional learning in educational settings. It represents the collaborative efforts of experts in education, psychology, and child development to empower improved well-being. CASEL focuses on building a strong foundation of self-understanding through self-awareness - identifying emotions, strengths, and weaknesses. Self-management skills empowers us to manage our emotions, impulses, and behaviors in a healthy way. Looking outward, social awareness fosters empathy and understanding of others' perspectives. Relationship skills equip us to build and maintain healthy connections, while responsible decision-making allows us to make choices with a clear consideration of consequences.

The CASEL framework aligns with the Brain Well-Being Model's efforts to promote positive mental health across the lifespan. Both cultivate responsive relationships, emotionally safe environments, and skill development; fostering a holistic approach that considers the interconnectedness of a community's emotional, social, and cognitive well-being. Through these elements, those exploring concepts of interconnectedness not only improve their attitudes about themselves and others but also experience reduced emotional distress and risky behaviors in all settings.

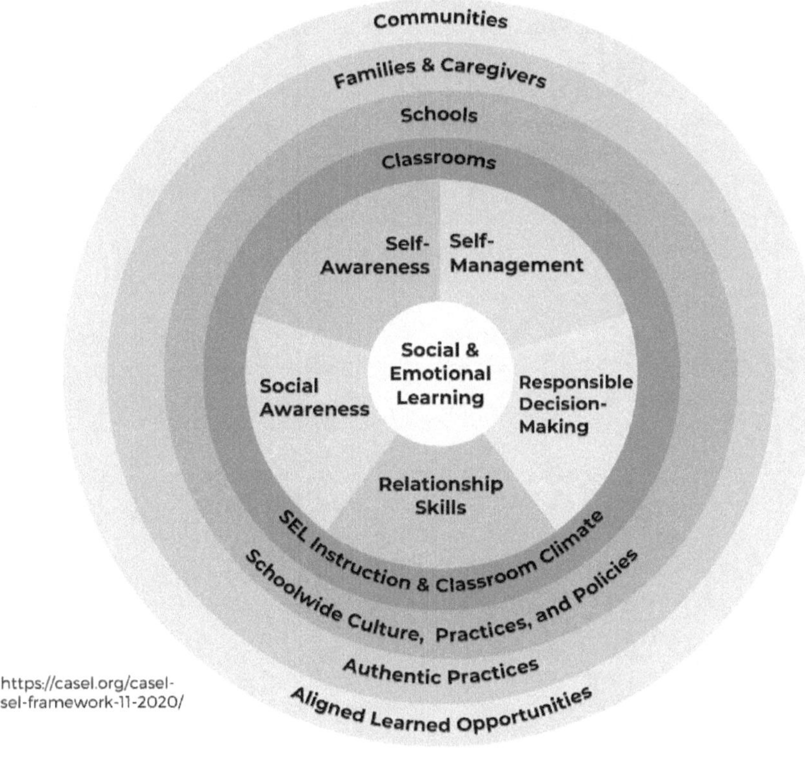

https://casel.org/casel-sel-framework-11-2020/

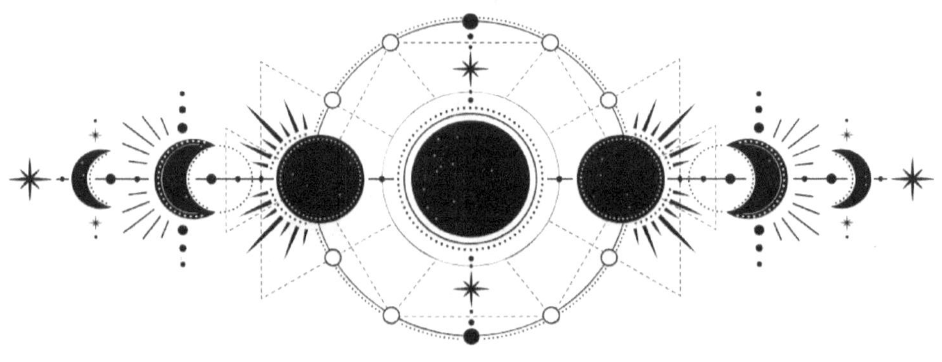

DATE:

SUNDAY
MONDAY
TUESDAY
WEDNESDAY
THURSDAY
FRIDAY
SATURDAY

THIS WEEK I AM MANIFESTING...

ACTION STEPS

What will be done by the end of the week?

TIMELINE   By when? (Day/Month)

RESPONSIBILITIES

Who will complete the prioritized tasks?

RESOURCES

(A) Resources Available (B) Resources Needed

COMMUNICATION PLAN

Who/What/When/Where/How was it communicated?

POTENTIAL BARRIERS

What might cause resistance to the ACTION STEPS? How?

GO GET IT MANTRA...

Choose a useful quote, image, or statement to serve as mental motivation. We must be loving of self when we choose this mantra.

GOAL OF THIS MOMENT

TASK LIST

Write down 10 action items that will lead you to your goal.

ACCOMPLISHMENTS

Be loud, proud, and bold about the things we have been able to conquer this week. Cheer this moment, do a happy dance, and notice the tasks left behind, for they were always meant for next week's accomplishment section instead. Celebrate even the tiniest success and we will attract more.

HOW DOES YOUR BODY FEEL?

Take this moment to notice ourselves. Are we breathing? Notice if our bodies need to stretch, take a break, or get some fresh air. This accountability tool also serves to help us take care of ourselves. When needed, document exactly what you noticed from this moment and throughout this week. This will be useful to track stressors and triggers, which can be barriers to action steps.

🏅 SELF CARE CHECKLIST

- ☐ Take 10 Deep Breaths
- ☐ Move! (Walk, Yoga, Run, Strut)
- ☐ Listen to Your Favorite Music
- ☐ Aromatherapy Time-Out
- ☐ Indulge in a Favorite __________
- ☐ Scream Out Loud!
- ☐ __________________________

- ☐ __________________________
- ☐ __________________________
- ☐ __________________________
- ☐ __________________________
- ☐ __________________________
- ☐ __________________________
- ☐ __________________________

I AM...

FREE WRITE PAGE

Week 15

5 LOVE LANGUAGES

Love languages are a form of communication about how we each give and receive love. Feeling unloved, isolated, and lonely are initial triggers for depression and anxiety symptoms. Our relationships impact our well-being. When we understand how we show up and love in our relationships and how we hope others show up for us, we build enough awareness to better our interactions with others.

Learning about the 5 love languages can be a valuable tool for increasing our relational awareness. It can help us to understand our own needs and preferences, as well as those of others, when it comes to giving and receiving love. By identifying and communicating our love language to our partner, friends, or family, we can improve the quality of our relationships and deepen our connections with others. Understanding the love languages of those around us can also help us to be more mindful and intentional in our interactions, and to show our love in ways that are most meaningful to them. The benefits of learning about the 5 love languages include enhanced communication, deeper connection, and greater satisfaction in our relationships.

LEARN ABOUT THE 5 LOVE LANGUAGES

Take some time to research and learn about the 5 love languages: Words of Affirmation, Quality Time, Receiving Gifts, Acts of Service, and Physical Touch. You can read about them in the book *The 5 Love Languages* by Gary Chapman or visit the website fivelovelanguages.com. Consider which love language(s) resonate with you and think about the ways in which you prefer to give and receive love.

5 LOVE LANGUAGES

Words of Affirmation		**Encouragement, affirmations, appreciation, empathize, listen actively, praise, compliments** Send an unexpected note, text, or card. Genuinely encourage often by placing post-its around the house.
Physical Touch		**Non-verbal body language and touch to show love. Setting boundaries for touch you will and will not allow** Hug, kiss, hold hands, show physical affection often. Make intimacy a thoughtful priority by hugging or kissing parents/guardians when leaving.
Receiving Gifts		**Thoughtfulness, make your loved ones a priority, speak purposefully** Give thoughtful gifts and gestures. Small things matter in a big way, gift favorite snacks. Express gratitude when receiving a gift.
Quality Time		**Uninterrupted and focused conversations, one-on-one time, routine** Create special moments together like taking walks, cooking dinner with the family, engaging in game night.
Acts of Service		**Let them know you are wanting to help.** Do chores or make breakfast for your parents/guardians. Get out of your way to help alleviate their daily workload. Be there for a friend. Volunteer with your community.

Discover your love language® - the 5 love languages®. Discover Your Love Language® - The 5 Love Languages®. (n.d.). https://5lovelanguages.com/

5 LOVE LANGUAGES

*Calvin and Hobbes

TAKE THE FIVE LOVE LANGUAGES QUIZ

We need to know ourselves and have awareness of the type of love we require. Relational awareness allows us to share what we know about ourselves with others. Take the Five Love Languages Quiz:

www.5lovelanguages.com/quizzes/

SHARE YOUR LOVE LANGUAGE

Communicating with those important to us and sharing our love language helps with mental wellness. Practice using "I" statements.

"I feel happy..."
"I feel validated when..."
"I feel connected when..."
"I feel sad when..."

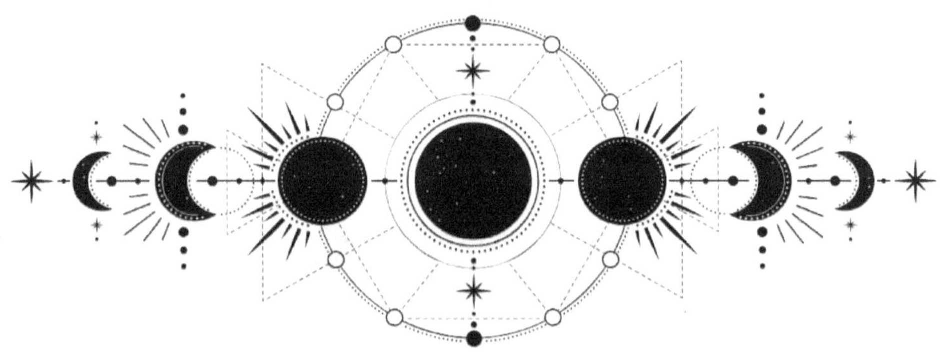

| SUNDAY |
| MONDAY |
| TUESDAY |
| WEDNESDAY |
| THURSDAY |
| FRIDAY |
| SATURDAY |

THIS WEEK I AM MANIFESTING...

ACTION STEPS

What will be done by the end of the week?

TIMELINE   By when? (Day/Month)

RESPONSIBILITIES

Who will complete the prioritized tasks?

RESOURCES

(A) Resources Available (B) Resources Needed

COMMUNICATION PLAN

Who/What/When/Where/How
was it communicated?

POTENTIAL BARRIERS

What might cause resistance
to the ACTION STEPS? How?

GO GET IT MANTRA...

Choose a useful quote, image, or statement to serve as mental motivation. We must be loving of self when we choose this mantra.

GOAL OF THIS MOMENT

TASK LIST

Write down 10 action items that will lead you to your goal.

ACCOMPLISHMENTS

Be loud, proud, and bold about the things we have been able to conquer this week. Cheer this moment, do a happy dance, and notice the tasks left behind, for they were always meant for next week's accomplishment section instead. Celebrate even the tiniest success and we will attract more.

HOW DOES YOUR BODY FEEL?

Take this moment to notice ourselves. Are we breathing? Notice if our bodies need to stretch, take a break, or get some fresh air. This accountability tool also serves to help us take care of ourselves. When needed, document exactly what you noticed from this moment and throughout this week. This will be useful to track stressors and triggers, which can be barriers to action steps.

⬢ SELF CARE CHECKLIST

- ☐ Take 10 Deep Breaths
- ☐ Move! (Walk, Yoga, Run, Strut)
- ☐ Listen to Your Favorite Music
- ☐ Aromatherapy Time-Out
- ☐ Indulge in a Favorite __________
- ☐ Scream Out Loud!
- ☐ __________

- ☐ __________
- ☐ __________
- ☐ __________
- ☐ __________
- ☐ __________
- ☐ __________
- ☐ __________

I AM...

FREE WRITE PAGE

PHYSICAL TOUCH

Learning about and practicing the Physical Touch love language can be a powerful way to enhance our relationships and deepen our connections with others. For those whose primary love language is Physical Touch, it is especially important to receive physical touch in order to feel loved and connected.

By incorporating more physical touch into our relationships, we can communicate love and affection in a way that is meaningful to our partners, friends, or family. Additionally, physical touch has been shown to have a variety of health benefits, including reducing stress and anxiety, increasing feelings of closeness and connection, and improving overall well-being.

EXPLORE PHYSICAL TOUCH

Spend some time this week exploring the Physical Touch love language. Think about the ways in which physical touch can communicate love and affection, and consider how you might incorporate more physical touch into your relationships. This could include hugging, holding hands, giving a shoulder rub, or simply sitting close to someone.

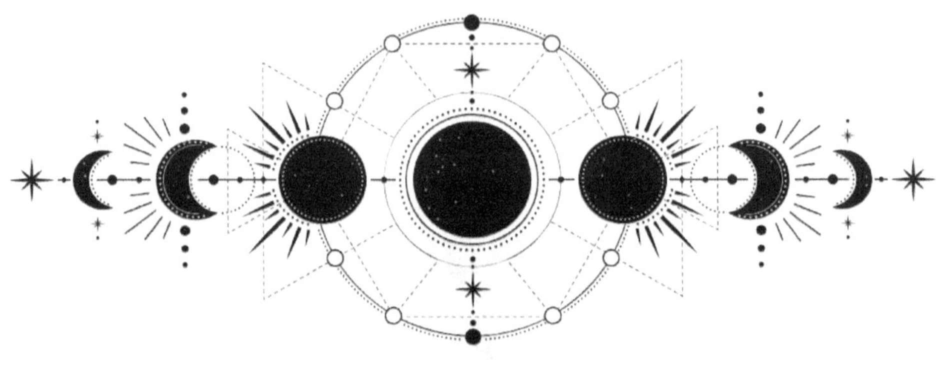

DATE:

SUNDAY
MONDAY
TUESDAY
WEDNESDAY
THURSDAY
FRIDAY
SATURDAY

THIS WEEK I AM MANIFESTING...

ACTION STEPS

What will be done by the end of the
week?

TIMELINE   By when? (Day/Month)

RESPONSIBILITIES

Who will complete the prioritized tasks?

RESOURCES

(A) Resources Available (B) Resources Needed

COMMUNICATION PLAN

Who/What/When/Where/How
was it communicated?

POTENTIAL BARRIERS

What might cause resistance
to the ACTION STEPS? How?

 Choose a useful quote, image, or statement to serve as mental motivation. We must be loving of self when we choose this mantra.

GOAL OF THIS MOMENT

⊛ TASK LIST

Write down 10 action items that will lead you to your goal.

____

____

____

____

____

____

____

____

____

ACCOMPLISHMENTS

Be loud, proud, and bold about the things we have been able to conquer this week. Cheer this moment, do a happy dance, and notice the tasks left behind, for they were always meant for next week's accomplishment section instead. Celebrate even the tiniest success and we will attract more.

HOW DOES YOUR BODY FEEL?

Take this moment to notice ourselves. Are we breathing? Notice if our bodies need to stretch, take a break, or get some fresh air. This accountability tool also serves to help us take care of ourselves. When needed, document exactly what you noticed from this moment and throughout this week. This will be useful to track stressors and triggers, which can be barriers to action steps.

⬤ SELF CARE CHECKLIST

- [ ] Take 10 Deep Breaths
- [ ] Move! (Walk, Yoga, Run, Strut)
- [ ] Listen to Your Favorite Music
- [ ] Aromatherapy Time-Out
- [ ] Indulge in a Favorite __________
- [ ] Scream Out Loud!
- [ ] __________________

- [ ] __________________
- [ ] __________________
- [ ] __________________
- [ ] __________________
- [ ] __________________
- [ ] __________________
- [ ] __________________

I AM...

FREE WRITE PAGE

WORDS OF AFFIRMATION

Practicing gratitude and expressing words of affirmation can be a powerful way to enhance our relationships and deepen our connections with others. For those whose primary love language is Words of Affirmation, it is especially important to receive verbal expressions of love and appreciation in order to feel loved and valued.

By practicing gratitude and expressing our appreciation for the people in our lives, we can communicate love and affection in a meaningful way to our partners, friends, or family. Additionally, research has shown that expressing gratitude can improve our mood, increase our feelings of well-being, and enhance our relationships with others.

PRACTICING GRATITUDE

Spend some time each day this week reflecting on the people in your life who have positively impacted you. Write down their names and some specific things you appreciate about them, then take the time to express your gratitude by sending them a note or message of appreciation. Use specific language to communicate what you admire about them and how they have impacted your life.

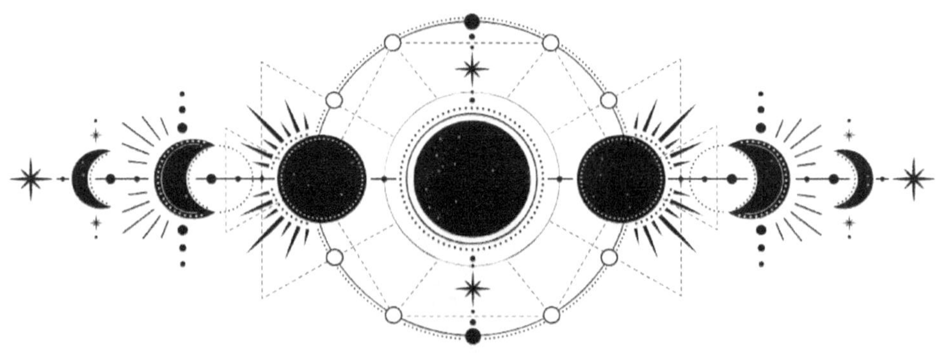

DATE:

SUNDAY
MONDAY
TUESDAY
WEDNESDAY
THURSDAY
FRIDAY
SATURDAY

THIS WEEK I AM MANIFESTING...

ACTION STEPS

What will be done by the end of the week?

TIMELINE   By when? (Day/Month)

RESPONSIBILITIES

Who will complete the prioritized tasks?

RESOURCES

(A) Resources Available (B) Resources Needed

COMMUNICATION PLAN

Who/What/When/Where/How
was it communicated?

POTENTIAL BARRIERS

What might cause resistance
to the ACTION STEPS? How?

GO GET IT MANTRA...

Choose a useful quote, image, or statement to serve as mental motivation. We must be loving of self when we choose this mantra.

GOAL OF THIS MOMENT

 ## TASK LIST

Write down 10 action items that will lead you to your goal.

ACCOMPLISHMENTS

Be loud, proud, and bold about the things we have been able to conquer this week. Cheer this moment, do a happy dance, and notice the tasks left behind, for they were always meant for next week's accomplishment section instead. Celebrate even the tiniest success and we will attract more.

HOW DOES YOUR BODY FEEL?

Take this moment to notice ourselves. Are we breathing? Notice if our bodies need to stretch, take a break, or get some fresh air. This accountability tool also serves to help us take care of ourselves. When needed, document exactly what you noticed from this moment and throughout this week. This will be useful to track stressors and triggers, which can be barriers to action steps.

⊛ SELF CARE CHECKLIST

☐ Take 10 Deep Breaths	☐ ___________________
☐ Move! (Walk, Yoga, Run, Strut)	☐ ___________________
☐ Listen to Your Favorite Music	☐ ___________________
☐ Aromatherapy Time-Out	☐ ___________________
☐ Indulge in a Favorite _________	☐ ___________________
☐ Scream Out Loud!	☐ ___________________
☐ ___________________	☐ ___________________

I AM...

FREE WRITE PAGE

ACTS OF SERVICE

For those whose primary love language is Acts of Service, actions speak louder than words. They feel most loved and appreciated when others go out of their way to do something helpful or thoughtful for them. By performing random acts of kindness for the people in our lives, we can communicate our love and appreciation in a way that is meaningful to them. This not only strengthens our relationships, but it can also enhance our own feelings of well-being and satisfaction. Studies have shown that performing acts of kindness can boost our mood and increase our levels of happiness and life satisfaction.

RANDOM ACTS OF KINDNESS

This week, focus on performing random acts of kindness for the people in your life. This could be something as simple as doing the dishes for your partner or offering to run an errand for a friend. Think about what you can do to make the lives of the people around you easier or more enjoyable.

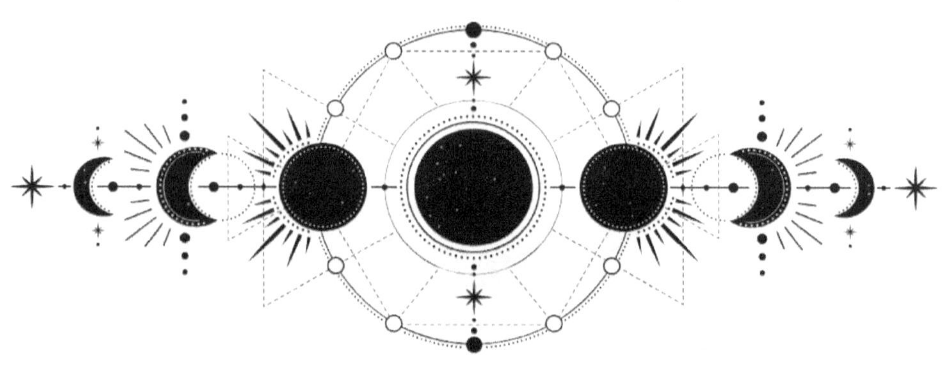

DATE:

SUNDAY

MONDAY

TUESDAY

WEDNESDAY

THURSDAY

FRIDAY

SATURDAY

THIS WEEK I AM MANIFESTING...

ACTION STEPS

What will be done by the end of the week?

TIMELINE   By when? (Day/Month)

RESPONSIBILITIES

Who will complete the prioritized tasks?

RESOURCES

(A) Resources Available (B) Resources Needed

COMMUNICATION PLAN

Who/What/When/Where/How
was it communicated?

POTENTIAL BARRIERS

What might cause resistance
to the ACTION STEPS? How?

GO GET IT MANTRA...

Choose a useful quote, image, or statement to serve as mental motivation. We must be loving of self when we choose this mantra.

GOAL OF THIS MOMENT

TASK LIST

Write down 10 action items that will lead you to your goal.

ACCOMPLISHMENTS

Be loud, proud, and bold about the things we have been able to conquer this week. Cheer this moment, do a happy dance, and notice the tasks left behind, for they were always meant for next week's accomplishment section instead. Celebrate even the tiniest success and we will attract more.

HOW DOES YOUR BODY FEEL?

Take this moment to notice ourselves. Are we breathing? Notice if our bodies need to stretch, take a break, or get some fresh air. This accountability tool also serves to help us take care of ourselves. When needed, document exactly what you noticed from this moment and throughout this week. This will be useful to track stressors and triggers, which can be barriers to action steps.

⊛ SELF CARE CHECKLIST

- ☐ Take 10 Deep Breaths
- ☐ Move! (Walk, Yoga, Run, Strut)
- ☐ Listen to Your Favorite Music
- ☐ Aromatherapy Time-Out
- ☐ Indulge in a Favorite __________
- ☐ Scream Out Loud!
- ☐ __________________

- ☐ __________________
- ☐ __________________
- ☐ __________________
- ☐ __________________
- ☐ __________________
- ☐ __________________
- ☐ __________________

I AM...

FREE WRITE PAGE

QUALITY TIME

For those whose primary love language is Quality Time, spending undivided attention with loved ones is the most valuable gift we can give them. It's not about how much time we spend with them, but the quality of that time.

By consciously unplugging and being present with the people in our lives, we can deepen our connections and show them how much we value their company. This can also enhance our feelings of connection, intimacy, and well-being. Studies have shown that spending quality time with loved ones can boost our mental health and increase our levels of happiness and life satisfaction.

UNPLUGGED TIME TOGETHER

This week, make a conscious effort to spend quality time with the people in your life without any distractions. This means putting away your phones, turning off the TV, and just being fully present in the moment with each other. You could go for a walk, have a game night, or simply sit and chat over a cup of tea.

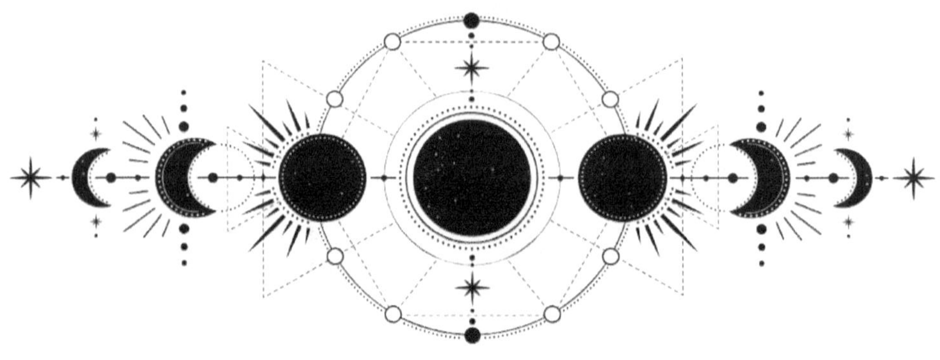

DATE:

| SUNDAY |
| MONDAY |
| TUESDAY |
| WEDNESDAY |
| THURSDAY |
| FRIDAY |
| SATURDAY |

THIS WEEK I AM MANIFESTING...

ACTION STEPS

What will be done by the end of the week?

TIMELINE   By when? (Day/Month)

RESPONSIBILITIES

Who will complete the prioritized tasks?

RESOURCES

(A) Resources Available (B) Resources Needed

COMMUNICATION PLAN

Who/What/When/Where/How
was it communicated?

POTENTIAL BARRIERS

What might cause resistance
to the ACTION STEPS? How?

GO GET IT MANTRA...

Choose a useful quote, image, or statement to serve as mental motivation. We must be loving of self when we choose this mantra.

GOAL OF THIS MOMENT

 ## TASK LIST

Write down 10 action items that will lead you to your goal.

ACCOMPLISHMENTS

Be loud, proud, and bold about the things we have been able to conquer this week. Cheer this moment, do a happy dance, and notice the tasks left behind, for they were always meant for next week's accomplishment section instead. Celebrate even the tiniest success and we will attract more.

HOW DOES YOUR BODY FEEL?

Take this moment to notice ourselves. Are we breathing? Notice if our bodies need to stretch, take a break, or get some fresh air. This accountability tool also serves to help us take care of ourselves. When needed, document exactly what you noticed from this moment and throughout this week. This will be useful to track stressors and triggers, which can be barriers to action steps.

SELF CARE CHECKLIST

- ☐ Take 10 Deep Breaths
- ☐ Move! (Walk, Yoga, Run, Strut)
- ☐ Listen to Your Favorite Music
- ☐ Aromatherapy Time-Out
- ☐ Indulge in a Favorite __________
- ☐ Scream Out Loud!
- ☐ __________________

- ☐ __________________
- ☐ __________________
- ☐ __________________
- ☐ __________________
- ☐ __________________
- ☐ __________________
- ☐ __________________

I AM...

FREE WRITE PAGE

MATERIAL GIFTS

For those whose primary love language is Material Gifts, the act of giving and receiving tangible items is an important way to express and receive love. However, it's important to remember that material gifts are just one of many ways to show love and appreciation and should never be a relationship's sole focus.

By taking time to reflect on what kinds of gifts we appreciate and enjoy giving, we can better understand our needs and preferences and those of the people we care about. This can help us to make more meaningful and thoughtful gift choices and to approach gift-giving in a way that aligns with our values and priorities. Additionally, it can also help us to appreciate the non-material aspects of our relationships and to cultivate a deeper sense of connection and intimacy with our loved ones.

GIVING AND RECEIVING

This week, think about material gifts' role in your relationships. Take some time to reflect on what kinds of gifts you appreciate receiving and why, as well as what kinds of gifts you enjoy giving and why. Then, try to incorporate these insights into your interactions with the people in your life.

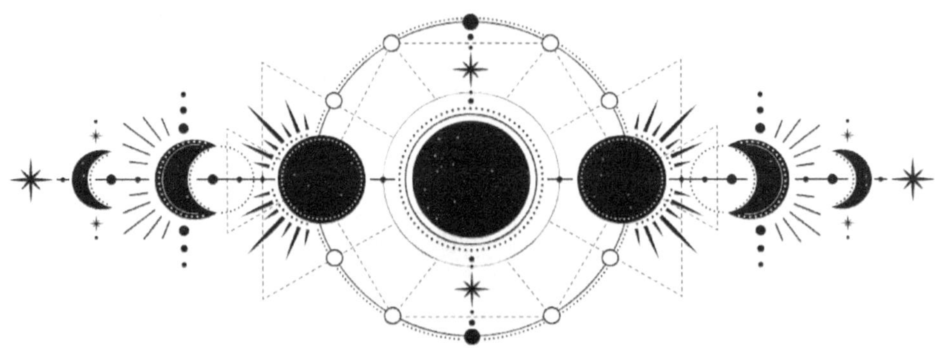

| SUNDAY |
| MONDAY |
| TUESDAY |
| WEDNESDAY |
| THURSDAY |
| FRIDAY |
| SATURDAY |

THIS WEEK I AM MANIFESTING...

ACTION STEPS

What will be done by the end of the week?

TIMELINE   By when? (Day/Month)

RESPONSIBILITIES

Who will complete the prioritized tasks?

RESOURCES

(A) Resources Available (B) Resources Needed

COMMUNICATION PLAN

Who/What/When/Where/How was it communicated?

POTENTIAL BARRIERS

What might cause resistance to the ACTION STEPS? How?

GO GET IT MANTRA...

Choose a useful quote, image, or statement to serve as mental motivation. We must be loving of self when we choose this mantra.

GOAL OF THIS MOMENT

⬥ TASK LIST

Write down 10 action items that will lead you to your goal.

ACCOMPLISHMENTS

Be loud, proud, and bold about the things we have been able to conquer this week. Cheer this moment, do a happy dance, and notice the tasks left behind, for they were always meant for next week's accomplishment section instead. Celebrate even the tiniest success and we will attract more.

HOW DOES YOUR BODY FEEL?

Take this moment to notice ourselves. Are we breathing? Notice if our bodies need to stretch, take a break, or get some fresh air. This accountability tool also serves to help us take care of ourselves. When needed, document exactly what you noticed from this moment and throughout this week. This will be useful to track stressors and triggers, which can be barriers to action steps.

⊛ SELF CARE CHECKLIST

- ☐ Take 10 Deep Breaths
- ☐ Move! (Walk, Yoga, Run, Strut)
- ☐ Listen to Your Favorite Music
- ☐ Aromatherapy Time-Out
- ☐ Indulge in a Favorite __________
- ☐ Scream Out Loud!
- ☐ __________

- ☐ __________
- ☐ __________
- ☐ __________
- ☐ __________
- ☐ __________
- ☐ __________
- ☐ __________

I AM...

FREE WRITE PAGE

Week 21

A SCARCITY MINDSET IN FINANCIAL MATTERS

A scarcity mindset is a belief that there is never enough of something - in this case, money - to go around. This mindset can lead to feelings of fear, anxiety, and stress around financial matters and can make it difficult to make decisions about spending, saving, and investing. A scarcity mindset can also make it harder to appreciate the good things that you already have in your life, as it can create a sense of constant striving and dissatisfaction. By identifying and challenging your scarcity beliefs, and practicing gratitude and abundance, you can cultivate a more positive and empowered mindset around money and financial matters.

Identify Your Scarcity Beliefs: **Take some time to reflect on** your financial beliefs and attitudes. Write down any beliefs you have about money and financial security, including any negative beliefs or fears that you may hold. For example, you might believe that there is never enough money to go around, that money is hard to come by, or that you will never be able to save enough for retirement.

Challenge Your Scarcity Beliefs: Once you have identified your scarcity beliefs, try to challenge them by examining the evidence that supports them. Ask yourself whether these beliefs are really true, or whether they are based on assumptions or past experiences that may no longer be relevant. Look for evidence that contradicts your scarcity beliefs, and try to reframe your thinking around abundance and possibility.

Practice Gratitude: Gratitude can be a powerful antidote to scarcity thinking. Take some time each day to focus on the things that you are grateful for, whether they are material possessions or intangible blessings like good health, supportive relationships, or fulfilling work. Cultivating a mindset of gratitude can help you to feel more content and satisfied with what you already have, and can reduce the urge to constantly strive for more.

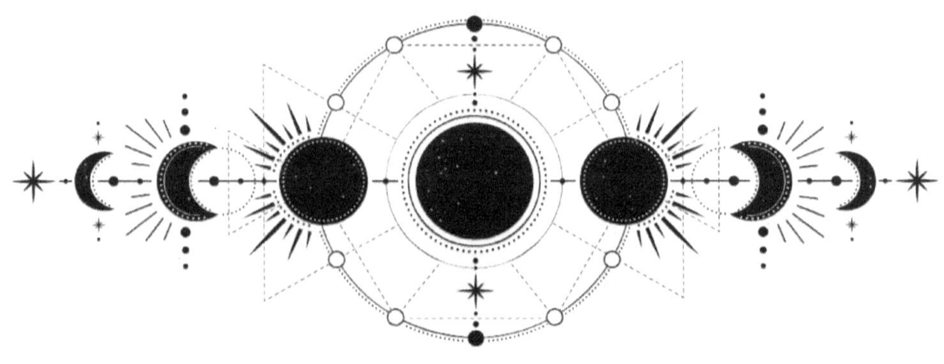

DATE:

SUNDAY	
MONDAY	
TUESDAY	
WEDNESDAY	
THURSDAY	
FRIDAY	
SATURDAY	

THIS WEEK I AM MANIFESTING...

ACTION STEPS

What will be done by the end of the week?

TIMELINE   By when? (Day/Month)

RESPONSIBILITIES

Who will complete the prioritized tasks?

RESOURCES

(A) Resources Available (B) Resources Needed

COMMUNICATION PLAN

Who/What/When/Where/How
was it communicated?

POTENTIAL BARRIERS

What might cause resistance
to the ACTION STEPS? How?

GO GET IT MANTRA...

Choose a useful quote, image, or statement to serve as mental motivation. We must be loving of self when we choose this mantra.

GOAL OF THIS MOMENT

TASK LIST

Write down 10 action items that will lead you to your goal.

ACCOMPLISHMENTS

Be loud, proud, and bold about the things we have been able to conquer this week. Cheer this moment, do a happy dance, and notice the tasks left behind, for they were always meant for next week's accomplishment section instead. Celebrate even the tiniest success and we will attract more.

HOW DOES YOUR BODY FEEL?

Take this moment to notice ourselves. Are we breathing? Notice if our bodies need to stretch, take a break, or get some fresh air. This accountability tool also serves to help us take care of ourselves. When needed, document exactly what you noticed from this moment and throughout this week. This will be useful to track stressors and triggers, which can be barriers to action steps.

⊛ SELF CARE CHECKLIST

- [ ] Take 10 Deep Breaths
- [ ] Move! (Walk, Yoga, Run, Strut)
- [ ] Listen to Your Favorite Music
- [ ] Aromatherapy Time-Out
- [ ] Indulge in a Favorite __________
- [ ] Scream Out Loud!
- [ ] __________

- [ ] __________
- [ ] __________
- [ ] __________
- [ ] __________
- [ ] __________
- [ ] __________
- [ ] __________

I AM...

FREE WRITE PAGE

Week 22

4 PRIMARY BARRIERS TO WELL-BEING

When it comes to well-being, there are several common barriers that can prevent individuals from feeling their best. These include distractibility, loneliness, negative self-talk, and lack of purpose or meaning. Let's take a closer look at each of these barriers and how they can impact our overall well-being.

Distractibility: In today's world, it's easy to get distracted by social media, work, or other responsibilities. This can prevent us from being fully present in the moment and can lead to feelings of overwhelm and stress.

Activity: One way to combat distractibility is to practice mindfulness. Try setting aside a few minutes each day to sit quietly and focus on your breath. Notice any thoughts or distractions that arise and gently bring your attention back to your breath.

Loneliness: Social isolation and loneliness can have a negative impact on our mental health and well-being, leading to feelings of sadness and disconnection.

Activity: Connect with others by joining a club, volunteering, or attending social events. Reach out to friends or family members you haven't spoken to in a while and make plans to catch up.

Negative Self-Talk: Negative self-talk can be a major barrier to well-being, as it can impact our self-esteem and overall mood.

Activity: Practice self-compassion by treating yourself with kindness and understanding. Challenge negative thoughts by reframing them in a more positive light.

Lack of Purpose/Meaning: Feeling like our lives lack purpose or meaning can leave us feeling unfulfilled and unhappy.

Activity: Take some time to reflect on what brings you joy and fulfillment. Set goals and make a plan to work towards them, whether through a career change, volunteering, or pursuing a new hobby.

Addressing these common barriers to well-being can improve our overall quality of life and cultivate greater feelings of happiness, fulfillment, and connection.

COMMON SYMPTOMS OF
MENTAL ILLNESS

- Changes in sleep
- New onset of guilt
- Changes in energy level
- Changes in concentration or task completion
- Changes in appetite
- Changes in motivation
- Thoughts of suicide
- Feeling guilty, worthless, or helpless
- Losing interest in hobbies or activities that used to be enjoyable
- Irritability/anger

PREVENTATIVE STRATEGIES

- Build a self-care routine
- Be aware of stressors/red flags
- Journal, blog, listen to music
- Talk-Therapy (to peers/counselor)
- Take up a new hobby/learn a skill
- Move your body, dance, take a walk, get some sun, hug someone, read, breathe, take a pause
- Engage in creating something: art, garden, music, poetry, film, business

IMMEDIATE STRATEGIES

1. Identify resources (medical, school, community)

2. Talk to a professional when you need a higher level of care; meaning feeling too overwhelmed or considering self-harm

3. Talk to someone trusted to decrease isolation and feelings of loneliness. Build a support system

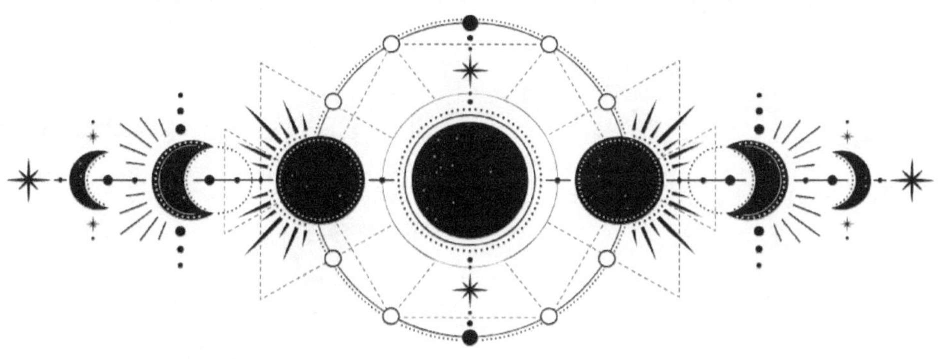

DATE:

SUNDAY
MONDAY
TUESDAY
WEDNESDAY
THURSDAY
FRIDAY
SATURDAY

THIS WEEK I AM MANIFESTING...

ACTION STEPS

What will be done by the end of the week?

TIMELINE   By when? (Day/Month)

RESPONSIBILITIES

Who will complete the prioritized tasks?

RESOURCES

(A) Resources Available (B) Resources Needed

COMMUNICATION PLAN

Who/What/When/Where/How
was it communicated?

POTENTIAL BARRIERS

What might cause resistance
to the ACTION STEPS? How?

 Choose a useful quote, image, or statement to serve as mental motivation. We must be loving of self when we choose this mantra.

GOAL OF THIS MOMENT

 **TASK LIST**

Write down 10 action items that will lead you to your goal.

ACCOMPLISHMENTS

Be loud, proud, and bold about the things we have been able to conquer this week. Cheer this moment, do a happy dance, and notice the tasks left behind, for they were always meant for next week's accomplishment section instead. Celebrate even the tiniest success and we will attract more.

HOW DOES YOUR BODY FEEL?

Take this moment to notice ourselves. Are we breathing? Notice if our bodies need to stretch, take a break, or get some fresh air. This accountability tool also serves to help us take care of ourselves. When needed, document exactly what you noticed from this moment and throughout this week. This will be useful to track stressors and triggers, which can be barriers to action steps.

⊛ SELF CARE CHECKLIST

- ☐ Take 10 Deep Breaths
- ☐ Move! (Walk, Yoga, Run, Strut)
- ☐ Listen to Your Favorite Music
- ☐ Aromatherapy Time-Out
- ☐ Indulge in a Favorite __________
- ☐ Scream Out Loud!
- ☐ __________________

- ☐ __________________
- ☐ __________________
- ☐ __________________
- ☐ __________________
- ☐ __________________
- ☐ __________________
- ☐ __________________

I AM...

FREE WRITE PAGE

 GARDENING AS SELF-CARE

Gardening is a great self-care activity that offers many benefits for both physical and mental health. By spending time outdoors and engaging in the task of tending to plants, gardening can help reduce stress and anxiety, improve mood and creativity, enhance physical health, and promote mindfulness.

Additionally, gardening allows individuals to connect with nature, which has been shown to have a positive impact on mental health and well-being. Whether you have a large backyard garden or a small window box, taking the time to care for plants can be a rewarding and relaxing experience that contributes to a greater sense of self-care and personal fulfillment.

GARDENING ACTIVITY

Choose a plant: Select a plant that you'd like to care for. It could be a flower, herb, or vegetable plant that you find appealing or would enjoy growing.

Prepare a pot: Get a pot that is large enough for the plant you've chosen. Add a layer of rocks or gravel at the bottom to aid in drainage. Then, fill the pot with soil that is suitable for the type of plant you've chosen.

Plant the seedling: Follow the instructions for planting your seedling. Make sure to gently remove the plant from its container and loosen any tangled roots before planting it in the pot.

Water and care for the plant: Give your new plant a good drink of water and place it in an area that gets the right amount of light and temperature. Check the soil regularly and water as needed. Take note of any changes in the plant's health, such as wilting or discoloration, and adjust your care accordingly.

Enjoy the benefits: As your plant grows, take the time to appreciate its progress and the work you've put into caring for it. Enjoy the beauty of the plant. Spending time tending to your plant can be a wonderful form of self-care that provides many benefits for your overall well-being.

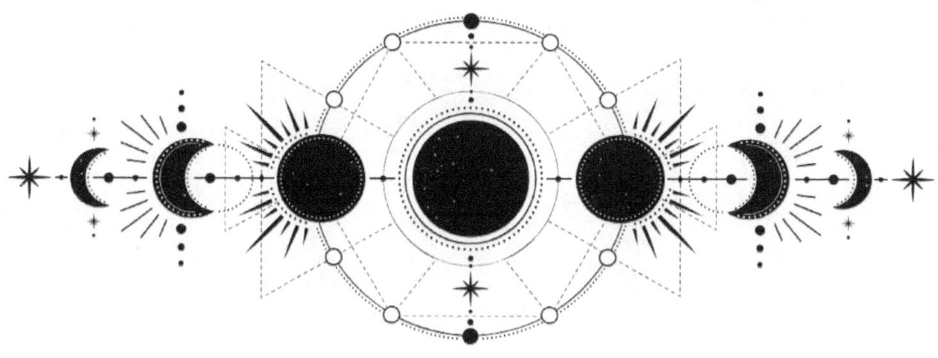

DATE:

SUNDAY
MONDAY
TUESDAY
WEDNESDAY
THURSDAY
FRIDAY
SATURDAY

THIS WEEK I AM MANIFESTING...

ACTION STEPS

What will be done by the end of the week?

TIMELINE   By when? (Day/Month)

RESPONSIBILITIES

Who will complete the prioritized tasks?

RESOURCES

(A) Resources Available (B) Resources Needed

COMMUNICATION PLAN

Who/What/When/Where/How
was it communicated?

POTENTIAL BARRIERS

What might cause resistance
to the ACTION STEPS? How?

GO GET IT MANTRA...

Choose a useful quote, image, or statement to serve as mental motivation. We must be loving of self when we choose this mantra.

GOAL OF THIS MOMENT

⬤ TASK LIST

Write down 10 action items that will lead you to your goal.

ACCOMPLISHMENTS

Be loud, proud, and bold about the things we have been able to conquer this week. Cheer this moment, do a happy dance, and notice the tasks left behind, for they were always meant for next week's accomplishment section instead. Celebrate even the tiniest success and we will attract more.

HOW DOES YOUR BODY FEEL?

Take this moment to notice ourselves. Are we breathing? Notice if our bodies need to stretch, take a break, or get some fresh air. This accountability tool also serves to help us take care of ourselves. When needed, document exactly what you noticed from this moment and throughout this week. This will be useful to track stressors and triggers, which can be barriers to action steps.

⊛ SELF CARE CHECKLIST

- ☐ Take 10 Deep Breaths
- ☐ Move! (Walk, Yoga, Run, Strut)
- ☐ Listen to Your Favorite Music
- ☐ Aromatherapy Time-Out
- ☐ Indulge in a Favorite __________
- ☐ Scream Out Loud!
- ☐ __________

- ☐ __________
- ☐ __________
- ☐ __________
- ☐ __________
- ☐ __________
- ☐ __________
- ☐ __________

I AM...

FREE WRITE PAGE

Week 24

MENTAL HEALTH BENEFITS OF EXERCISE

Regular exercise offers many mental health benefits, including reduced symptoms of depression and anxiety, improved mood, and increased self-esteem.

Exercise also helps to reduce stress and promote better sleep, which can have a positive impact on overall mental health. One activity that you can try to reap the mental health benefits of exercise is a brisk walk.

ACTIVITY

Take a brisk walk outdoors for 20-30 minutes, focusing on your breath and the sensations in your body as you move. This can be a great way to clear your mind and reduce stress, while also getting some physical activity. If you're feeling up to it, you can also try jogging or running to increase the intensity of your workout.

Remember to stay hydrated and stretch before and after your walk to prevent injury. By incorporating regular exercise into your routine, you can improve your overall mental health and well-being.

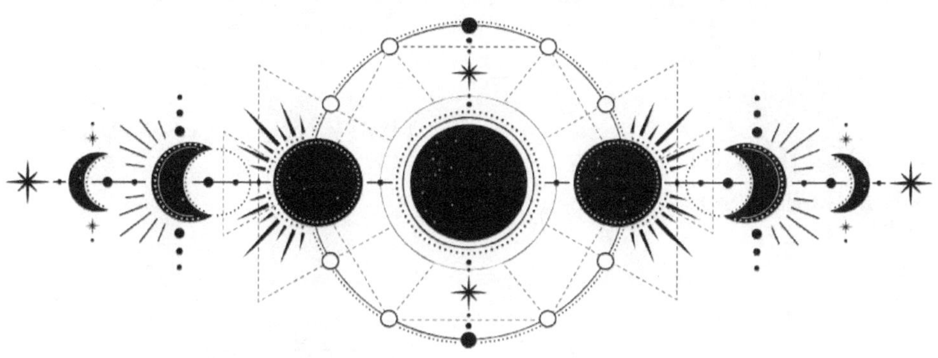

DATE:

SUNDAY
MONDAY
TUESDAY
WEDNESDAY
THURSDAY
FRIDAY
SATURDAY

THIS WEEK I AM MANIFESTING...

ACTION STEPS

What will be done by the end of the week?

TIMELINE   By when? (Day/Month)

RESPONSIBILITIES

Who will complete the prioritized tasks?

RESOURCES

(A) Resources Available (B) Resources Needed

COMMUNICATION PLAN

Who/What/When/Where/How
was it communicated?

POTENTIAL BARRIERS

What might cause resistance
to the ACTION STEPS? How?

Choose a useful quote, image, or statement to serve as mental motivation. We must be loving of self when we choose this mantra.

GOAL OF THIS MOMENT

 TASK LIST

Write down 10 action items that will lead you to your goal.

ACCOMPLISHMENTS

Be loud, proud, and bold about the things we have been able to conquer this week. Cheer this moment, do a happy dance, and notice the tasks left behind, for they were always meant for next week's accomplishment section instead. Celebrate even the tiniest success and we will attract more.

HOW DOES YOUR BODY FEEL?

Take this moment to notice ourselves. Are we breathing? Notice if our bodies need to stretch, take a break, or get some fresh air. This accountability tool also serves to help us take care of ourselves. When needed, document exactly what you noticed from this moment and throughout this week. This will be useful to track stressors and triggers, which can be barriers to action steps.

⊛ SELF CARE CHECKLIST

- ☐ Take 10 Deep Breaths
- ☐ Move! (Walk, Yoga, Run, Strut)
- ☐ Listen to Your Favorite Music
- ☐ Aromatherapy Time-Out
- ☐ Indulge in a Favorite __________
- ☐ Scream Out Loud!
- ☐ __________

- ☐ __________
- ☐ __________
- ☐ __________
- ☐ __________
- ☐ __________
- ☐ __________
- ☐ __________

I AM...

FREE WRITE PAGE

Week 25

THE SECRET TO BEHAVIOR CHANGE

The secret to behavior change lies in making small, sustainable changes over time. When we try to make big changes all at once, it can be overwhelming and difficult to maintain.

By focusing on small, achievable goals, we can build momentum and create lasting change. One activity that can help with behavior change is habit tracking.

ACTIVITY

Choose one small habit that you want to develop, such as drinking more water or going for a daily walk. Create a habit tracker by drawing a grid with the days of the week and the habit you want to track at the top.

Each day that you complete the habit, mark a check or an X in the corresponding box. Over time, you'll be able to see your progress and build confidence in your ability to create lasting change. As the habit becomes more ingrained, you can add new habits to your tracker and continue building toward your goals.

By focusing on small, achievable changes and tracking your progress over time, you can make lasting behavior change and improve your overall well-being. Remember to be patient with yourself and celebrate your successes along the way.

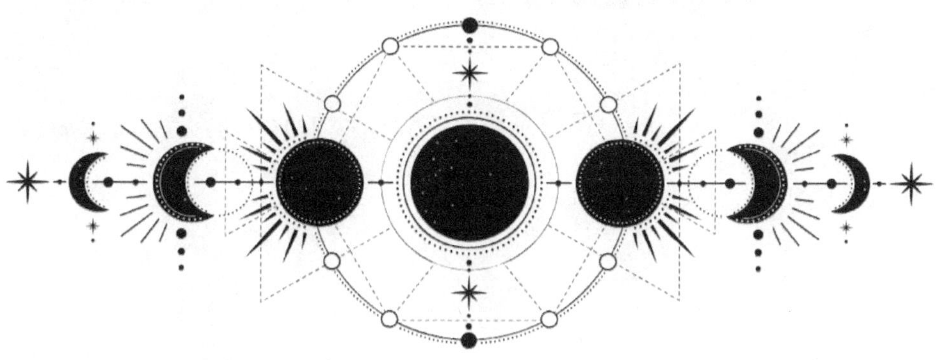

DATE:

SUNDAY
MONDAY
TUESDAY
WEDNESDAY
THURSDAY
FRIDAY
SATURDAY

THIS WEEK I AM MANIFESTING...

ACTION STEPS

What will be done by the end of the week?

TIMELINE   By when? (Day/Month)

RESPONSIBILITIES

Who will complete the prioritized tasks?

RESOURCES

(A) Resources Available (B) Resources Needed

COMMUNICATION PLAN

Who/What/When/Where/How was it communicated?

POTENTIAL BARRIERS

What might cause resistance to the ACTION STEPS? How?

GO GET IT MANTRA...

Choose a useful quote, image, or statement to serve as mental motivation. We must be loving of self when we choose this mantra.

GOAL OF THIS MOMENT

 TASK LIST

Write down 10 action items that will lead you to your goal.

ACCOMPLISHMENTS

Be loud, proud, and bold about the things we have been able to conquer this week. Cheer this moment, do a happy dance, and notice the tasks left behind, for they were always meant for next week's accomplishment section instead. Celebrate even the tiniest success and we will attract more.

HOW DOES YOUR BODY FEEL?

Take this moment to notice ourselves. Are we breathing? Notice if our bodies need to stretch, take a break, or get some fresh air. This accountability tool also serves to help us take care of ourselves. When needed, document exactly what you noticed from this moment and throughout this week. This will be useful to track stressors and triggers, which can be barriers to action steps.

⊛ SELF CARE CHECKLIST

- [ ] Take 10 Deep Breaths
- [ ] Move! (Walk, Yoga, Run, Strut)
- [ ] Listen to Your Favorite Music
- [ ] Aromatherapy Time-Out
- [ ] Indulge in a Favorite __________
- [ ] Scream Out Loud!
- [ ] __________

- [ ] __________
- [ ] __________
- [ ] __________
- [ ] __________
- [ ] __________
- [ ] __________
- [ ] __________

I AM...

FREE WRITE PAGE

Week 26

REACH THAT UPPER LEVEL OF THE GLOW

To reach that upper level of the "glow," it's important to take care of our physical, mental, and emotional well-being. One activity that can help to promote a healthy glow is practicing yoga.

ACTIVITY

Find a quiet space where you can practice yoga, either at home or in a studio. Begin with some gentle stretching to warm up your body, then move into a series of yoga poses that feel good for you.

Focus on your breath and the sensations in your body as you move, letting go of any stress or tension. End your practice with a few minutes of relaxation or meditation, allowing yourself to fully relax and release any remaining tension.

Yoga can help to improve flexibility, strength, and balance, while also reducing stress and promoting relaxation. By incorporating regular yoga practice into your routine, you can promote a healthy glow from the inside out, and improve your overall well-being. Remember to listen to your body and practice within your own limits, adjusting the intensity of your practice as needed.

Our *'Feel Well' Self-Care Yoga Deck* is a great tool to help you practice your daily yoga poses and to get inspired with affirmations and journal prompts. Purchase yours at manifestapothecary.com.

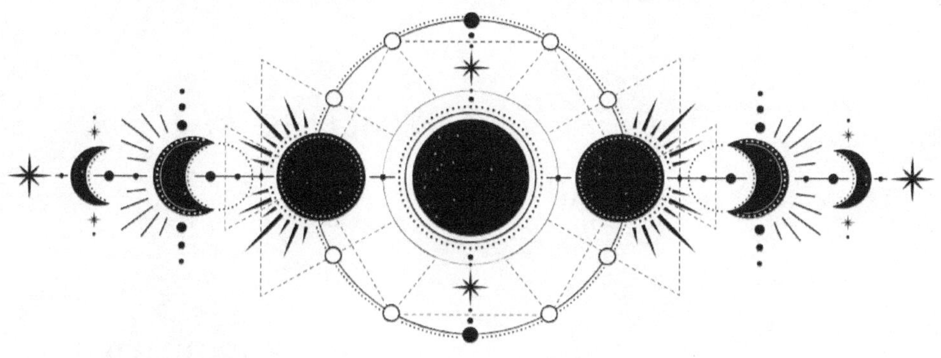

| SUNDAY |
| MONDAY |
| TUESDAY |
| WEDNESDAY |
| THURSDAY |
| FRIDAY |
| SATURDAY |

THIS WEEK I AM MANIFESTING...

ACTION STEPS

What will be done by the end of the
week?

TIMELINE   By when? (Day/Month)

RESPONSIBILITIES

Who will complete the prioritized tasks?

RESOURCES

(A) Resources Available (B) Resources Needed

COMMUNICATION PLAN

Who/What/When/Where/How
was it communicated?

POTENTIAL BARRIERS

What might cause resistance
to the ACTION STEPS? How?

GO GET IT MANTRA...

Choose a useful quote, image, or statement to serve as mental motivation. We must be loving of self when we choose this mantra.

GOAL OF THIS MOMENT

TASK LIST

Write down 10 action items that will lead you to your goal.

ACCOMPLISHMENTS

Be loud, proud, and bold about the things we have been able to conquer this week. Cheer this moment, do a happy dance, and notice the tasks left behind, for they were always meant for next week's accomplishment section instead. Celebrate even the tiniest success and we will attract more.

HOW DOES YOUR BODY FEEL?

Take this moment to notice ourselves. Are we breathing? Notice if our bodies need to stretch, take a break, or get some fresh air. This accountability tool also serves to help us take care of ourselves. When needed, document exactly what you noticed from this moment and throughout this week. This will be useful to track stressors and triggers, which can be barriers to action steps.

⊛ SELF CARE CHECKLIST

- ☐ Take 10 Deep Breaths
- ☐ Move! (Walk, Yoga, Run, Strut)
- ☐ Listen to Your Favorite Music
- ☐ Aromatherapy Time-Out
- ☐ Indulge in a Favorite _____________
- ☐ Scream Out Loud!
- ☐ _____________

- ☐ _____________
- ☐ _____________
- ☐ _____________
- ☐ _____________
- ☐ _____________
- ☐ _____________
- ☐ _____________

I AM...

FREE WRITE PAGE

THE PROCESS OF COMPLETION

The Process of Completion: Goals Attained or Renewed

Over 26 weeks, we have focused on a goal, project, or commitment. It could have been anything from conquering a fitness challenge to mastering a new skill or overcoming a habit that didn't serve. Now, let's break it down and explore if we have met the challenge, or need to start over and try again. Both are valid and important parts of the experience of growth. If we want something, we must try and try again until it is ours.

As we close out 26 weeks of manifesting the best life for ourselves; we invite some processing about the following:

<table>
<tr><td align="center">INITIAL VISION</td></tr>
</table>

- What got you started on this 26-week journey?
- Did you follow the course of tracking your original expectations and objectives?

____

____

____

____

____

PROGRESS AND CHALLENGES

- What milestones did you hit?
- What obstacles did you encounter, and how did you overcome them?
- What changed for the better during the journey?

LESSONS LEARNED

- Any surprises about yourself or the process?
- What are the main takeaways to carry forward?

- How did you realize it was time to move forward/close out this process of self-exploration?
- How did you tie up loose ends?
- Will you be continuing for another 26-weeks to give yourself more time on the same goal(s) or will you establish a new goal and work towards that on your own time or for another 26 weeks?

Explore and document your thoughts to inform your actions. This action planner may be able to serve as excellent accompaniment to your reparative/healing work with a psychotherapist, life coach or trusted partner to empower increased well-being and insight.

____

____

____

____

____

____

____

____

____

____

____

- Reaching a goal or transitioning can stir up various emotions. How did you feel... accomplished, relieved, or maybe a bit melancholic?
- How did you handle these feelings?

LOOKING AHEAD AND TAKING STOCK

- Now that this 26-week chapter is closing, what's next?
- Any new goals or opportunities in sight?
- How can you use the lessons learned to fuel future endeavors?

By pondering these points, you'll gather valuable insights to propel yourself toward even greater achievements! As you finalize your process of completion, explore concepts such as a growth mindset, mindful affirmations, and types of self-care. Practice vision boarding, tracking resolutions and goals and maybe even write a letter to your future self.

Happy Manifesting!

DISCOVER THE MAGIC
OF A GROWTH MINDSET!

A growth mindset is all about believing in your ability to improve and grow. It means understanding that intelligence and skills can be developed through dedication and hard work. With a growth mindset, you can overcome challenges, learn from mistakes, and achieve great things!

CHALLENGE YOURSELF

With a growth mindset, you know that challenges are opportunities for growth. Don't be afraid to take on new and difficult tasks. Step out of your comfort zone, set goals, and watch yourself grow.

LEARN FROM MISTAKES

Mistakes are valuable learning opportunities, not something of which to be ashamed. With a growth mindset, you see mistakes as stepping stones to success. When you make a mistake, take a deep breath, learn from it, and try again.

BELIEVE IN YOUR POTENTIAL

With a growth mindset, you understand that intelligence and talents can be developed over time. Keep pushing yourself, stay positive, and believe in your ability to achieve anything you set your mind to. You have unlimited potential.

EMBRACE EFFORT AND PERSISTANCE

With a growth mindset, you know that effort and perseverance are the keys to achieving your goals. Stay determined, work hard, and celebrate the progress you make along the way!

SPEAK IT. WRITE IT.
WILL IT. CLAIM IT.

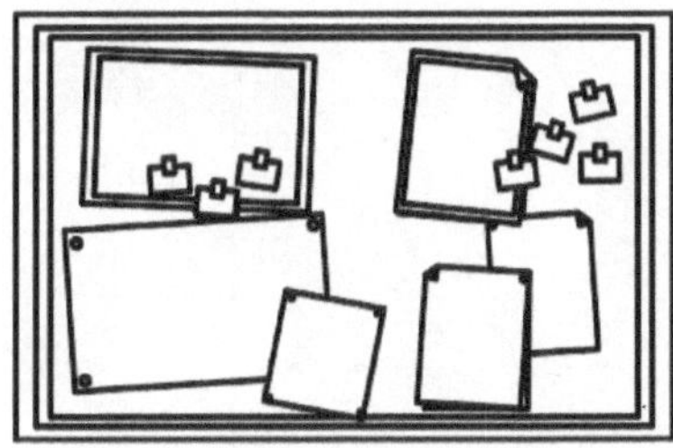

"Speak it. Write it. Will it. Claim it." is a powerful mantra that can help us to manifest our dreams and goals. By speaking our desires into existence, writing them down, visualizing them, and taking action toward them, we can create a powerful intention that can help us to achieve what we want.

One activity that can help us to put this into practice is creating a vision board.

ACTIVITY

Gather some magazines, scissors, glue, and a poster board or paper. Spend some time thinking about what you want to manifest in your life, whether it's a new job, a relationship, or improved health. Look through the magazines for images and words that resonate with your goals, and cut them out. Arrange the images and words on your poster board or paper, creating a visual representation of your desires. Hang your vision board somewhere where you'll see it every day, and take action toward your goals.

By creating a visual representation of our desires and taking action toward them, we can harness the power of the "speak it, write it, will it, claim it" mantra to achieve our dreams. Remember to stay focused and take consistent action toward your goals, trusting that the universe will support you along the way.

VISION BOARD

travel

GOALS

FAMILY

hobbies

RELATIONSHIPS

CAREER

HEALTH

money

Do more of what you love

Mindful Affirmations

I am worthy of love and acceptance.

Today, I prioritize my peace.

I embrace my uniqueness.

My body deserves respect.

I attract abundance effortlessly.

I trust my journey.

I release the past, embrace the present.

Love flows to me freely.

My mind is positive and empowering.

Success is my birthright.

I let go, embrace potential.

The universe supports my dreams.

I am a powerful creator.

I am deserving of self-care and compassion.

Today, I choose to honor my needs.

I love and accept myself completely.

My body is a temple of health and vitality.

I attract positive experiences into my life.

I believe in my abilities and strengths.

I forgive myself and others, freeing my spirit.

Love surrounds me in all forms.

My thoughts are filled with positivity and abundance.

I am unstoppable in achieving my goals.

I release fear and step into courage.

The universe conspires in my favor.

I am a magnet for joy and fulfillment.

self-care

/ˌselfˈker/ noun

the practice of taking action to preserve or improve one's own health.

GO ON A MINDFUL WALK	TAKE A BUBBLE BATH	COOK A HEALTHY MEAL	SIGN UP FOR A NEW HOBBY	GO SOMEWHERE FANCY
TAKE A SOCIAL MEDIA BREAK	30 MINUTE MEDITATION	PLAN A PRETTY PICNIC	CALL AN OLD FRIEND	EXPLORE NATURE
DANCE IN THE LIVING ROOM	PLAN A VACATION	GO TO BED 1 HOUR EARLIER	BUY YOURSELF A GIFT	START A NEW BOOK
TRY AROMATHERAPY	SAY YOUR AFFIRMATIONS	AT- HOME FACIAL	ORGANIZE YOUR CLOSET	GET A MASSAGE
PRACTICE BREATHWORK	COMPLIMENT YOURSELF	LISTEN TO 432 HZ MUSIC	CREATE SOMETHING	BUY YOURSELF FLOWERS
LIGHT SOME CANDLES	DO SOME YOGA	WATCH THE SUNRISE	GO FOR A RUN	WATCH A FEEL GOOD MOVIE

RESOLUTIONS AND GOALS CHECKLIST

HABITS

- ○
- ○
- ○
- ○
- ○

THINGS TO LEARN

- ○
- ○
- ○
- ○
- ○

HEALTH RESOLUTIONS

- ○
- ○
- ○
- ○
- ○

CAREER AND MONEY

- ○
- ○
- ○
- ○
- ○

MATERIAL THINGS

- ○
- ○
- ○
- ○
- ○

PERSONAL DEVELOPMENT

- ○
- ○
- ○
- ○
- ○

Letter to my
future self

Dear _____________________________ ,

Signed: ___________________________

Date: ___________________________

Works Cited

Ackerman, Courtney E. (2023, June 3) What Is Self-Awareness? (+5 Ways to Be More Self-Aware). https://sites.bu.edu/impact/previous-issues/impact-summer-2022/the-power-of-storytelling/

Casel's SEL framework. CASEL. (2021, August 11). https://casel.org/casel-sel-framework-11-2020/

Discover your love language® - the 5 love languages®. Discover Your Love Language® - The 5 Love Languages®. (n.d.). https://5lovelanguages.com/

Duval & Wicklund, 1972 - Ackerman, Courtney E. (2023, June 3) What Is Self-Awareness? (+5 Ways to Be More Self-Aware). https://positivepsychology.com/self-awareness-matters-how-you-can-be-more-self-aware/

Enos, S. (2022, July 21). Brand archetypes:. DEKSIA. https://deksia.com/blog/strategy/brand-archetypes

The feeling wheel: A tool for expanding awareness of emotions and … (n.d.). https://journals.sagepub.com/doi/abs/10.1177/036215378201200411

Home. BROWN GIRL TRAUMA. (2023, August 24). https://browngirltrauma.com/

Jo Nash, Ph. D. (2023, April 19). How to set healthy boundaries &; build positive relationships. PositivePsychology.com. https://positivepsychology.com/great-self-care-setting-healthy-boundaries/

Leonard, K. (2022, May 11). The Ultimate Guide to S.M.A.R.T. goals. Forbes. https://www.forbes.com/advisor/business/smart-goals/

Mette Miriam Böll, Peter Senge. Introduction to the Compassionate Systems Framework in Schools. Ackerman, Courtney E. (2023, June 3) What Is Self-Awareness? (+5 Ways to Be More Self-Aware). https://positivepsychology.com/self-awareness-matters-how-you-can-be-more-self-aware/

Montano, C. F. (2017, April 2). A Japanese technique for overcoming laziness. Bright Side - Inspiration. Creativity. Wonder. https://brightside.me/articles/a-japanese-technique-for-overcoming-laziness-11255/

The power of storytelling to facilitate human connection and learning. The Power of Storytelling to Facilitate Human Connection and Learning | IMPACT. (n.d.). https://sites.bu.edu/impact/previous-issues/impact-summer-2022/the-power-of-storytelling/

Nakeya T. Fields, LCSW, PPSE, Registered Play Therapist-Supervisor, Trauma Informed Yoga Therapist (LCS 25754/RPT-S1619)

Nakeya T. Fields, LCSW is a mental health entrepreneur, author, speaker, motivator, educator and advocate. She lives in Los Angeles, California and is a proud Mommy to Amare and Nova. She loves pottery, hand-building in particular, and loves to travel. Self-care is a preferred lifestyle choice as there has never been a spa day that didn't have her name on it.

Nakeya is the Founder of the Therapeutic Play Foundation, a nonprofit that seeks to build a healthier, more resilient world through empowerment, education and play. Nakeya is also the CEO of Innovative Wellness Consulting which supports organizations and educational facilities with professional development, wellness based activities and mental health based curriculum and programming.

Nakeya is passionate about empowering others, especially fellow mental health professionals. She recognizes the unique challenges they face and actively seeks to nurture and encourage them on their journey to success. This includes helping them monetize their expertise through customized coaching and consultation, potentially incorporating Manifest Apothecary's wellness product line as a complementary resource for their clients alongside the Manifest it! Action Planner.

Further, Nakeya acts as a program development consultant to develop progressive health and wellness programs that incorporate mindfulness, play and creative modalities within educational, corporate and community driven organizations. She also provides in-service seminars/workshops and is available for book signings, yoga and sound healing, speaking engagements, and consultation.

Thank You

I'm so grateful to the people who helped me create this book. I couldn't have done it without them!

To my partners in thought and execution, Chell Le Carter and Amanda Gonzalez, thanks for always being there to implement my vision and empower the ideas forward. To my son, Amare, thanks for being my heartbeat behind the drum of my passion and drive. To my parents, Lisa, Big Danny, and Wayne, for gifting me with love and support and confidence in my power. To my Nana, for being my number 1 fan because you knew I was yours. To my team at Therapeutic Play Foundation and Innovative Wellness Consulting, thanks for believing in me and helping me to birth this book.

To my fellow dreamers, beasts, and advocates in the field of mental health, wellness, and people empowerment, thanks for your stimulating discussions and collaboration.

And to my family and friends, thanks for putting up with me while I was writing this book and building a legacy of power through ritual and routine. You guys stuck by me through every passionate lecture and I'm so lucky to have you to inspire me and motivate me to keep pushing for innovative ideas that manifest into reality.

Finally, I want to thank you, the reader. I wish you joy as you take action toward manifesting the life you deserve and demand. I expect that this book will teach you something new or make you think in a different way that guides you toward your most authentic self. And so it is. Ase.

With good energy,

Nakeya T. Fields, LCSW, PPSE, Registered-Play Therapist-Supervisor
The Feel Well Coach

READY TO PRACTICE MANIFESTING?

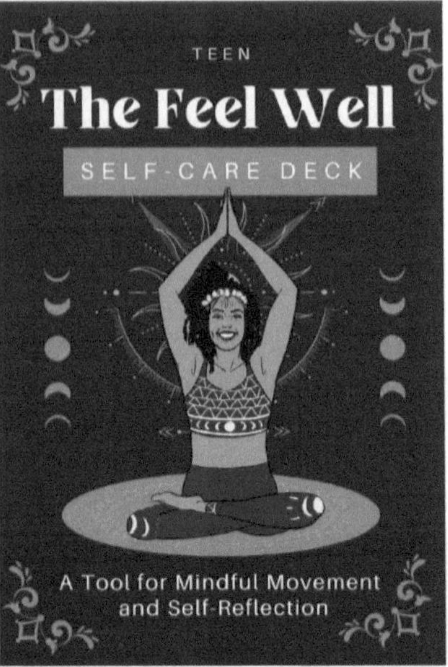

MANIFESTAPOTHECARY.COM

A vital part of taking action to manifest our best selves is having the tools to help build routine. In order for wellness to occur, we have to think about it and notice opportunities to take action.

The practice of moving the body in conjunction with breath is a great entry point into the practice of mindfulness and empathy. Allowing ourselves a moment of pause with our bodies can help us train our brain to better recover from moments of dysregulation.

We start to learn what our bodies feel like when feeling safe and relaxed and what our bodies feel like when we are not. Focus training, breathing, and movement are scientifically proven ways to regulate the body's nervous system when it is disrupted by stress.

The Feel Well Self-Care Yoga Deck offers strategies developed to support your journey. It empowers self-awareness, growth, gratitude, confidence, compassion, stronger boundaries, and a sense of peace through yoga poses, journaling prompts, inspirational quotes, affirmations, and more.

Purchase today at **manifestapothecary.com**.

About Atmosphere Press

Founded in 2015, Atmosphere Press was built on the principles of Honesty, Transparency, Professionalism, Kindness, and Making Your Book Awesome. As an ethical and author-friendly hybrid press, we stay true to that founding mission today.

If you're a reader, enter our giveaway for a free book here:

SCAN TO ENTER
BOOK GIVEAWAY

If you're a writer, submit your manuscript for consideration here:

SCAN TO SUBMIT
MANUSCRIPT

And always feel free to visit Atmosphere Press and our authors online at atmospherepress.com. See you there soon!